6   Finance

7   Human Resources

8   Operations Management

1 BUSINESS IN CONTEMPORARY SOCIETY

Business Activity

Business activity involves using the four factors of production to produce goods and services which people require in order to obtain the things they want.

1.1 Business Cycle

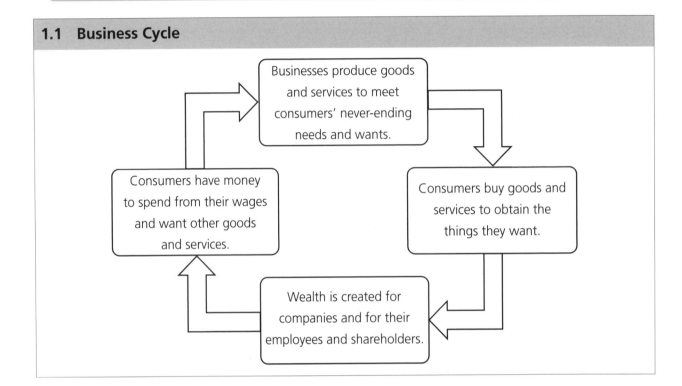

1.2 Factors of Production

Land
Land means the natural resources which businesses use (eg plot of land, coal, diamonds, forests, water, wood).

Labour
Labour means the workforce of a business.

Capital
Capital means the tools, machinery and equipment that a business owns or controls. It also includes the finance (money) that the owner has invested in the business.

Enterprise
Enterprise means the business ideas that an entrepreneur or owner has on how to use land, labour and capital in her/his business.

1.3 Sectors of Activity

Businesses can be grouped into sectors according to the types of product they produce or service they provide.

Primary sector
Businesses in this category grow products or extract resources from the ground (eg mining, farming, forestry).

Secondary sector
Businesses in this category manufacture products (eg shipbuilding, construction, factories).

Tertiary sector
Businesses in this category do not produce a product but provide a service (eg shops, hotels, window cleaners, banks).

Since the 1960s the secondary sector in the UK has declined significantly, resulting in fewer manufacturing firms. There has been a significant reduction in steel factories, shipbuilding and mills. This has been due to changes in consumer demand, lack of competitiveness amongst UK manufacturers, increasing competition from abroad, lack of investment in manufacturing, the effects of UK government policies and trade union practices.

The tertiary (service) sector has grown at the expense of the primary and secondary sectors in the UK. For example, whilst farming, mining, shipbuilding and steel production have declined significantly over the last 40 years in Scotland, businesses in the service sector (eg in tourism, finance and retailing) have seen considerable growth.

1.4 Types of Business Organisations

Type of Organisation	Characteristics
Sole Trader	**Definition** A sole trader is a one-owner business (ie owned and controlled by one person). Most small local businesses are sole traders (eg hairdressers).

Advantages	Disadvantages
All profits kept by owner.	Owner has unlimited liability.
Owner has complete control over all decisions.	Available finance is restricted.
Owner can choose hours of work/holidays.	Owner has no one to share decisions/problems with.
More personal service offered to customers.	Owner has no one to share workload with.
Very easy to set up.	Work stops if owner is ill/on holiday.

Finance is available from: owner's savings, business's retained profits, bank loan, bank overdraft, government grants, trade credit, and debt factoring.

Possible **objectives** might include: to survive; to maximise profits; to improve owner's personal status; to have a good image in the community.

1.4 Types of Business Organisations (cont.)

Type of Organisation	Characteristics
Partnership	**Definition** A partnership is a business with 2 to 20 partners – people who own and control the business together. The partners have to produce a Partnership Agreement which states each partner's rights and procedures to be followed when any partner joins, leaves or dies.

Advantages ➕	Disadvantages ➖
Partners can bring in different areas of expertise.	Partners have unlimited liability.
More finance available.	Profits have to be shared between partners.
Workload can be shared.	Partners may disagree.
Partners in a stronger position than a sole trader to raise finance from lenders.	If one partner dies or leaves, a new Partnership Agreement needs to be set up.

Finance is available from: partners' savings, partnership profits from previous years, inviting a new partner to join, bank loan, bank overdraft, government grants, trade credit, and debt factoring.

Possible **objectives** might include the same objectives as those of a sole trader.

Type of Organisation	Characteristics
Private Limited Company	**Definition** A private limited company is a company whose shares are owned privately (ie are not available to the public on the Stock Market). It has a minimum of one shareholder. It is owned by the shareholder(s) and run by a director or a board of directors. A shareholder can be a director. There must be a minimum of one director and one company secretary (who keeps all shareholder and company records). The company has to produce a Memorandum of Association and Articles of Association that state the company's details, responsibilities of directors and shareholders' rights. Private limited companies tend to be family businesses. Arnold Clark and Baxters are two examples of private limited companies which are family owned.

Advantages ➕	Disadvantages ➖
Shareholders have limited liability.	Profits shared amongst more people.
Control of company not lost to outsiders.	There is, as with a Partnership, a legal process in setting up the company.
More finance can be raised from shareholders and lenders.	Shares cannot be sold to the public. Therefore raising finance is more difficult than for a public limited company.
Significant experience and expertise from shareholders and directors.	Firm has to abide by the requirements of the Companies Act.
	Firm must publish annual accounts.

Finance is available from: company profits from previous years, inviting a new shareholder to join, bank loan, bank overdraft, government grants, trade credit, and debt factoring.

Possible **objectives** might include: to maximise profits; to grow; to have a strong status; to have the highest possible sales revenue.

Type of Organisation	Characteristics
Public Limited Company	**Definition** A public limited company (plc) is a company whose shares are available for purchase by the public on the Stock Market. There must be a minimum of two shareholders and £50,000 share capital. A Memorandum of Association and Articles of Association that state the company's details, responsibilities of directors and shareholders' rights have to be produced. Shareholders own a plc. A board of directors control the company. BT, Vodafone, Stagecoach and Celtic FC are all examples of plcs.

Advantages	Disadvantages
Huge amounts of finance can be raised. Plcs often dominate their markets. Easy to borrow money from lenders due to their large size.	Set-up costs of company may be high (eg they may have to produce top quality, detailed prospectuses and arrange underwriting). Must abide by the Companies Act. No control over who buys shares. Must publish annual accounts.

Finance is available from: company profits from previous years, selling shares to the public, bank loan, bank overdraft, issue debentures, government grants, trade credit, and debt factoring.

Possible **objectives** might include: to maximise profits; to expand output; to grow; to have a higher sales revenue than in previous years; to dominate their market; to have a strong image.

Some plcs are very large, global companies. Where a plc has manufacturing plants in more than one country it is classed as a multinational. ICI, Honda and Shell are all multinationals. By being a multinational a company may:
- take advantage of economies of scale
- avoid restrictions on the number of products imported into a country
- avoid restricting legislation in its home country
- receive tax advantages and grants from other governments.

1.5 Franchises

Type of Organisation	Characteristics
Franchise 	**Definition** A franchise is a business agreement that allows one business (the franchisee) to use another business's name and sell the other business's products or services (eg The Body Shop, McDonald's, Benetton and The British School of Motoring). He/she pays the franchiser (the business whose name is being used) a percentage of annual turnover or a set royalty each year to use its name and sell its products/services. The franchisee and franchiser can set up in any type of business, i.e. a sole trader, partnership, etc.

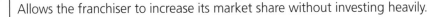

Advantages to the franchiser

Allows the franchiser to increase its market share without investing heavily.

Provides a reliable revenue (the franchiser will receive a % of the profits or a set royalty payment each year).

Risks and uncertainty are shared between the franchiser and the franchisee.

Advantages to the franchisee	Disadvantages to the franchisee
Franchiser may advertise nationally, therefore little advertising needs to be done by the franchisee.	Products, selling prices and store layout may be dictated, stifling franchisee initiative.
The risk of business failure is reduced as the business already has a good trading record and is often already established in its market.	A royalty payment or % of profits has to be paid to franchiser.
The franchiser may carry out training and administration.	The franchiser might not renew the franchise after a certain time.

1.6 Voluntary and Charitable Organisations

Type of Organisation	Characteristics
Charities	The government regulates the activities of charities and keeps a Register of Charities. Charities are exempt from paying some taxes. They are often run by professionals who work for the charity. Examples of charities include Oxfam and Cancer Research UK. **Finance** is available from: donations from the public and companies; government grants; Lottery grants; profits from their own shops; sale of goods through mail order; raffles, fêtes and jumble sales. Possible **objectives** might include: to provide a service; to relieve poverty; to fund research into various medical conditions.

1.6 Voluntary and Charitable Organisations (cont.)

Type of Organisation	Characteristics
Voluntary Organisations	Voluntary organisations are run and staffed by volunteers. Examples include the Scouts, youth clubs and some sports clubs. They bring together people with similar interests. They are run by a committee of elected volunteers. These organisations can raise **finance** by applying for grants from the Lottery, Sports Council or local authorities. They may also charge a fee to become a member of their organisation or to use their facilities.

1.7 Public Sector Organisations

These are organisations that are owned and controlled by local or central government

Type of Organisation	Characteristics
Local Government Organisations 	Local government/local unitary authorities/local councils provide a range of services including local education, recreation, housing and refuse collection. Local councils are set up by central government and are run on its behalf by locally elected councillors. The day-to-day running of services is organised by employees of the council. A local council aims to meet local needs. It provides services that might be unprofitable if provided by private firms (eg library services). Possible **objectives** might include: to meet local needs; to provide a wide range of services; to make cost savings; to stick to agreed budgets. **Finance** comes from central government, from business rates and from council tax. Councils also charge for some services such as leisure centre entrances and parking.
Central Government Organisations	Westminster and the Scottish Parliament provide important national services. Services are provided by government departments such as Treasury, Defence, Trade and Industry, Health and Transport. Possible **objectives** might include: to provide a service; to improve society; to make effective use of funds; to make effective use of taxes. **Finance** mainly comes from taxation. Policies and direction of departments come from elected politicians. Departments are run by employed civil servants.

1.7 Public Sector Organisations (cont.)

Type of Organisation	Characteristics
Public Corporations	These are companies that are owned by central government. A government minister appoints a chairperson and board of directors to run the company on the government's behalf. Public corporations include the BBC and Royal Mail Group. Possible **objectives** might include: to provide a quality service; to make best use of funds; to be better than rivals; to serve the public interest. Public corporations receive grants from the government and also raise **finance** from the public. The BBC charges the public for a TV licence and also sells videos/merchandise for programmes it produces. **Privatisation** Over the last 20 years, many public corporations have been privatised (sold) by the government to become public limited companies, with their shares traded on the Stock Market. Examples include British Airways, Scottish Power and British Telecom. Governments sold these companies because: • selling public corporations generates huge amounts of income for the government's Treasury. • some public corporations were poorly managed and not profitable. The government felt that, if sold off, they would become more competitive and profitable in the future. • the government wanted to increase share ownership and make the public have an interest in the success of companies and the economy. However: • Public corporations were often sold off too cheaply. • Privatisation has not always led to greater competition.

1.8 Objectives

Objectives are goals (aims) which organisations have. Objectives are crucial to structured decision-making. Having objectives often motivates people in the organisation. Typical corporate objectives include:

- survival
- growth
- sales revenue maximisation
- provision of a service

- profit maximisation
- social and ethical responsibility
- specific managerial objectives.

Objectives depend on: size of organisation, age of organisation, state of the economy and whether the organisation is in the public or the private sector.

Objectives may not be achieved due to: competition; environment; law; political situation; demands of shareholders, owners or society.

1.8 Objectives (cont.)

Sales Revenue Maximisation

To achieve as much sales revenue as possible. This is popular with sales staff who receive bonuses or salaries according to sales made.

Profit Maximisation

Where a private sector organisation aims to make as much profit as possible.

Growth

Many organisations aim to grow. A firm can aim to be more competitive, dominate the market and control prices. Growth can reduce the chance of failure.

Managerial Objectives

Managers in an organisation often have their own specific aims (eg to increase their own salary, or to improve their position and responsibility).

Survival

Continuing to trade is vital especially for a new business, particularly when there is a recession, increased competition or reduced demand.

Image and Social Responsibility

Many organisations aim to have a good image and be responsible towards customers, employees and suppliers. For example, Marks & Spencer has been working to improve its image with younger customers.

Provision of a Service

A charity or local authority would have this objective.

Many organisations also have among their stated aims to provide equal opportunities and to eliminate discrimination. Many organisations also aim to be environmentally friendly.

1.9 Stakeholders

A stakeholder is a person, organisation or group that has an interest in the success of an organisation.

Internal Stakeholders in an organisation may include:

Owners	Managers
Shareholders	Volunteers
Employees	

External Stakeholders in an organisation may include:

Customers	Local community
Trade unions	Pressure groups
Suppliers	Donors
Bankers/lenders	Government

Stakeholder	Their Interest	Their Influence
Owners	They have invested time, effort and finance and taken a risk in setting it up – they want it to succeed and produce profits.	They can exert influence on an organisation by making decisions about how it is run (eg which staff to hire, and pricing of products).
Shareholders	They want the firm to be profitable to provide them with good dividends and improved share value.	They can exert influence on the firm by voting for particular directors and approving dividend payments at the AGM.

1.9 Stakeholders (cont.)

Stakeholder	Their Interest	Their Influence
Managers	They receive salaries and perhaps bonuses so they will want the organisation to be successful. They also want responsibility and status.	They make important decisions regarding hiring staff, product portfolio, etc, which may or may not be successful.
Employees	They want good salaries, job satisfaction, good working conditions and job security.	They can exert influence by the standard of their work and industrial relations (eg strikes).
Customers	They want best quality products from organisations at lowest prices.	Customers can choose to buy or not to buy an organisation's products or services. This influences the products and services an organisation makes/gives.
Government	It wants businesses to succeed as they provide jobs, generate wealth and provide government with finance through taxes.	Government can exert influence through legislation (eg Health and Safety laws, environmental laws). The government's economic policies also affect businesses (eg setting of interest rates and the government's inflation policy).
Suppliers	Suppliers want their customers to succeed to ensure their own success (eg by repeat custom).	They can exert influence by changing prices, credit periods and discounts offered.
Local Community	Organisations create employment and therefore generate wealth for an area. Local communities also have an environmental interest in the organisation (eg a desire to avoid noise, air and land pollution).	They can exert influence by petitioning companies or making complaints to their local authority.

Conflict between stakeholders

As stakeholders do not all have the same interest in an organisation, conflict may arise between different stakeholders. For example, a business may want to maximise profits, whereas its customers will want to buy goods at the lowest prices. A business may want to build a new factory, but the local community may object as it could harm their local environment. The owners of a business may want to close a factory to cut costs but employees will not want to lose their jobs.

1.10 Role of the Entrepreneur

> *An entrepreneur is an individual who develops a business idea and combines the factors of production (ie land, labour, capital and enterprise) in order to produce a product or provide a service.*

Entrepreneurs tend to be risk takers and use their initiative. They initially make all the business decisions from raising finance to hiring staff and so they have to be good decision-makers. Richard Branson (of Virgin Group), Anita Roddick (of The Body Shop), Tom Farmer (of Kwik-Fit) and Michelle Mone (of MJM International, makers of the Ultimo Bra) are all well-known entrepreneurs who each started with a small business and made it grow. Most entrepreneurs start as a small business and are responsible for all aspects of it – from marketing and production to dealing with suppliers. As the business grows, the role of the entrepreneur may alter as he/she will then have managers/employees to delegate responsibility to.

1.11 What is a Manager?

It is the responsibility of managers to ensure the organisation achieves its objectives.

Functions of managers

Planning	Setting a plan of action for the future
Organising	Collecting and arranging resources to meet plans
Commanding	Ensuring duties are done properly by informing staff of what they have to do
Co-ordinating	Having staff and resources organised to achieve the plan
Controlling	Making sure everything works according to the plan

Skills a manager requires

Interpersonal	The relationship a manager has with others (eg to lead, to encourage, to liaise, to motivate)
Informational	The collecting and passing on of information (eg gathering data, processing data and communicating)
Decisional	Making different kinds of decisions (eg solving problems, allocating resources)

1.12 Sources of Finance

Businesses can access many different sources of finance. The source of finance used depends on what finance is required for, and for how long it is required. Sources include: bank loan; overdraft; hire purchase; retained profits; share issues; debentures; venture capital; grants; trade credit; factoring; leasing; selling an asset.

Short-Term Sources of Finance	Advantages	Disadvantages
Bank Overdraft	A customer can arrange to take out more from their bank account than they have in it. It is simple to arrange. The amounts borrowed can vary up to an agreed limit and it is relatively cheap as interest is only charged on the actual amount borrowed for the number of days borrowed.	Can work out to be expensive if used for a long time. If the limit is exceeded, the facility may be withdrawn immediately and expensive charges incurred.
Trade Credit	Firms buy goods from suppliers and pay for them at a later date. This helps a business get through periods when cash flow is poor.	Discount for prompt payment is lost. If payment is made outwith the credit period, suppliers may be reluctant to sell more goods on credit.
Factoring	A business can sell its customer invoices to a factoring company for less than their value. This improves cash flow as advance payment of bills is made by the factor. The factor chases up the unpaid invoices, saving the company time and money doing this.	Factors tend to be interested only in large values and quantities of invoices as they charge per invoice and number of invoices to be collected. The business does not receive the full amount of the original invoice from the factor.
Sale of an Asset	Where a business sells off items that it owns to gain additional finance.	Usually only used as a last resort source of cash.
Grant	A source of finance from central or local government, the EU or enterprise agencies. It is often an incentive for a new business setting up or an inducement to set up business in a particular area of high unemployment.	They are one-off payments that once received are not usually repeated.
Retained Profits	Profits kept back from previous years can be used to purchase assets.	Companies that self-finance using retained profits often find it difficult to grow at the speed they would like.

Medium-Term Sources of Finance	Advantages ➕	Disadvantages ➖
Bank Loan	The bank agrees to lend money for a specific period of time, amount, purpose and agrees repayment instalments. This makes budgeting/planning easier as repayments are made in regular, fixed instalments.	Small businesses tend to pay higher interest rates.
Leasing	A business can rent vehicles or equipment from a leasing company. This can be used to avoid using up limited finance on an outright purchase. Leased equipment can be changed when obsolete.	The lessee does not own the equipment. Rental charges can build up over a long period of time – it may work out to have been less expensive to buy in the first place.
Hire Purchase	A deposit is made for a vehicle or equipment with the rest of the purchase price paid for in instalments. The cost is spread, making it easier to afford. The piece of equipment is owned by the company at the end of the instalment period.	The goods are owned by the finance company until the last instalment is paid. It is an expensive form of borrowing.

Long-Term Sources of Finance	Advantages ➕	Disadvantages ➖
Owner's Savings	This can reduce the amount to be borrowed if funds are needed. It allows the owners to keep control without bringing in other owners.	Once invested, owner's capital can be difficult to withdraw and the owner's capital is at risk if the business fails (if the owner has unlimited liability).
Share Issue	This source of finance is available to companies. Shareholders have limited liability. Shareholders usually receive an annual dividend in return for their investment. Very large sums can be raised.	The costs of issuing shares can be expensive and it is difficult to estimate an appropriate selling price of shares.
Debentures	This is a source of finance used by plcs. A debenture is a group of loans from individuals and/or other companies. Debenture holders receive fixed interest over the period of the loan and then receive the amount of the loan back at the end (eg after 25 years).	Debenture interest must be paid even if the business makes a loss. If the business fails, debenture holders have a right to sell its assets in order to have the loan repaid.
Venture Capital	Venture capitalists will often provide finance when banks decide a loan is too risky. Venture capitalists accept more risky loans.	Venture capitalists are usually only interested in very large loans. The fee for their services is often high and they often want part-ownership in exchange for finance.

1.13 Sources of Assistance

A new or existing business can turn to a variety of different organisations for support and assistance.

Business Start-up Scheme
Run by Enterprise Agencies on behalf of the government, this scheme gives a weekly allowance (money) to people who start up their own business.

Enterprise Fund
This is a government scheme that allows small businesses starting up to borrow money from a bank. The bank lends the money with the government guaranteeing part of the loan.

Local Enterprise Agency
These are government-funded organisations set up to help small businesses. They offer free advice, training courses and provide contacts.

The Prince's Trust
Gives advice, training and grants to young people starting a business.

Trade Associations
Provide advice in their area of business. Examples include the Association of British Travel Agents (ABTA) and the Institute of Plumbing.

Banks
Give advice on sources of finance and drawing up a business plan. Many produce a pack of information useful to small businesses.

Inland Revenue
Gives advice on taxation matters.

1.14 Methods of Growth

A business often grows by integrating with another to become larger and more powerful. If the integration is on equal terms, it is called a merger (eg Cadburys and Schweppes merged to form Cadbury Schweppes plc). If one firm takes control of another so that one is lost completely, it is called a takeover (eg Morrisons Supermarkets took over Safeway in 2003. All Safeway stores will be changed to Morrisons.) There are three types of integration:

1. Horizontal Integration
Firms producing the same type of product or providing the same type of service combine together (eg two florists merging). Goods/services become cheaper due to bulk buying and lower admin costs. These firms tend to dominate the market, compete against smaller firms and finally raise prices.

2. Vertical Integration
Firms at different stages of production in the same industry combine together (eg an oil refinery integrating with a petrol station).

Forward vertical integration occurs when a business takes over a customer. This allows a firm to increase profits and control supply and distribution of their product.

Backward vertical integration occurs when a business takes over a supplier. This gives a guaranteed source of stock. As stock will be cheaper, increased profits are possible.

3. Conglomerate (Diversification) Integration
This occurs when businesses operating in different markets merge. This reduces the risk of business failure. A firm may seek new opportunities if it fears loss of market share or competition. It makes a larger and more financially secure business.

De-integration

This occurs when a business cuts back on or sells minor areas of their business in order to concentrate on core areas. This also provides funds from selling off less profitable areas.

De-merger

This occurs when a business splits into two separate organisations to raise cash for investment. It concentrates its efforts on its core activities and cuts costs to make it more efficient. For example, BT Cellnet demerged in 2001 into two separate companies – BT and mmO$_2$. Mobile phone company O$_2$ is a brand of mmO$_2$.

Divestment

This occurs when a business sells its business assets or a subsidiary company to raise finance. For example, British Leyland sold Rover (one of its subsidiaries) to BMW in 1994.

Asset Stripping

This occurs when a business buys another and then sells off the profitable sections bit by bit, and closes down the loss-making sections. A business may be worth more when sold off bit by bit than for the sum of what it was purchased for. Asset stripping can sometimes happen following a hostile takeover.

Contracting out/Outsourcing

This involves one firm hiring another to supply parts or to do part of a job instead of the firm doing it themselves. A manufacturer may contract a delivery company to deliver goods rather than do it themselves. Commonly outsourced work includes printing, electrical work and catering. Businesses outsource work because they do not possess the specialist equipment or expertise for the task, or because they do not have enough staff, or if a rush order for an important customer is needed.

Management Buy-out and Buy-in

A Management Buy-out happens when top managers buy the business they work in from the current owners. The managers then own the business. Managers may wish to buy out the business to enable them to keep their jobs and to make the firm more efficient. The current owners may wish to sell the business to raise finance for themselves.

A Management Buy-in happens when a group of managers from outside the business takes over the business and runs it.

1.15 External Business Environment

A company ignores the external business environment at its peril. The external environment means those events that are outwith a company's control. All companies must react to changes in the external environment. They are summarised as PESTEC factors or pressures.

P	Political factors
E	Economic factors
S	Social factors
T	Technological factors
E	Environmental factors
C	Competitive factors

PESTEC Factor	Description
Political factors	UK and EU laws and political decisions affect every business in the UK. For example, governments have set laws which ban advertising tobacco on television and disallow shops to sell alcohol on Sunday mornings. Businesses must comply with laws or face heavy legal penalties. Government policy can affect businesses by the government placing orders (eg orders for new defence ships to shipbuilding yards); setting taxation rates; providing infrastructure such as roads, rail, schools, hospitals.
Economic factors	Inflation, exchange rates and interest rates all affect businesses. If sterling (the British currency) is high in comparison to other currencies, British manufacturers struggle to sell products abroad. If the interest rate is high, the cost of borrowing for expansion is high. If there is a recession then unemployment rises and consumers have less income which results in loss of sales for businesses. There is a rise in discounting and interest-free credit when there is a recession to encourage consumer spending.
Social factors	**Demographic changes** are movements in the size and distribution of the population. The following demographic changes have taken place over a period of time. Businesses take note of these to help them provide their customers with products that they want.

Demographic Change	Reaction of Business
The UK has a slow-growing population and an ageing one.	There has been a growth in products for the elderly. Some DIY stores now actively recruit older staff with practical DIY experience to assist customers.
The average number of children in a family has fallen below two.	There has been a growth in sales of smaller family cars.
The average age of a first-time mother is now 29 (it was 24 a decade ago).	Some businesses are now producing maternity products for more affluent first-time mothers.

PESTEC Factor	Description
Social factors (cont.)	**Socio-cultural changes** are changes in lifestyle and attitudes in society. | Socio-cultural Change	Reaction of Business | |---|---| | More women are now in work.	Supermarkets now sell more ready-made meals, stay open longer and provide internet shopping. | | Change in attitudes regarding divorce and couples living together.	Housebuilders now build smaller homes. | | Increased concern about animal welfare and the environment.	Car manufacturers make cars that give off lower emissions. | | People have more leisure time.	Growth in hotels and restaurants as more people eat out and take more holidays. | | Increased car ownership	Increase in out-of-town shopping centres | | Consumer tastes have changed to be more health conscious.	There has been a rise in sales of low-fat meals and bottled water.	
Technological factors	Firms must keep up with new technology or face losing customers, sales, and profits. For example, they use email, the internet and databases to attract customers. Some businesses also use new technology to reduce costs in production lines.
Environmental factors	Environmental factors could include storms, floods, pollution or noise. Some businesses have been severely affected by flooding in recent years. They have had to close and refurbish. This is an environmental weather event over which they have little control.
Competitive factors	Most businesses face competition that has an influence on the way they operate. For example, Littlewoods Football Pools was affected when the National Lottery was introduced, so had to alter its selling and promotional techniques.

2 BUSINESS INFORMATION AND INFORMATION TECHNOLOGY

Data

Data is a collection of facts or quantities that has been assembled in some formal manner with the objective of processing it into specific information.

Information

Information is data that has been processed into a form that assists decision-making and planning.

2.1 Sources of Information

Sources of Information	Strengths	Weaknesses
Primary Information has been researched directly by an organisation for its own purposes, usually by observation, interview or questionnaire.	Information gained is first-hand and should be correct for the purpose for which it was gathered.	Market research costs may be high. Research may be flawed (eg too small a sample; or leading questions used). Respondents may have lied. May be difficult to collect. May have researcher bias.
Secondary Information is gathered from published sources such as newspapers, textbooks, the internet and magazines.	Can be inexpensive and easy to access. A wide variety of sources of secondary information is available.	Information gathered for one purpose and then used for another may not be relevant. May have author bias. May be out of date. Is available to competitors.
Internal Information is data that has been taken from the organisation's internal records (eg financial records, personal data).	Accurate information can be gained once an organisation has been established for several years. Accurate records can help set and achieve targets by revealing past performance.	Costs of setting up and producing personnel and wages records may be high. New organisations may not have internal information to access. Accurate records need to be kept.
External Information is gathered from sources outside the organisation (eg from market research, government reports, newspapers, competitors' annual accounts).	Can give an organisation useful information about PESTEC factors.	Time-consuming and expensive to gather. May be out of date. Information gained may be unreliable or biased. Is available to competitors.

2.2 Types of Information

Type of Information	Description	Strengths and Weaknesses
written	Information in the form of text (eg letters, memos, reports, emails, minutes)	Good for passing on information to confirm verbal messages; good for passing on information to be kept and used later; easy to collect.
oral	Verbal and sound information (eg from telephone calls, presentations, meetings and conversations or discussions)	Good for providing advice and simple instructions. However, it is less formal than written information and can be easily forgotten.
Pictorial	Information in the form of pictures and photos	Used for passing on information that can be easily remembered, making documents more attractive and to emphasise a point. However, a relevant picture which effectively illustrates a point may be hard to find.
GRAPHICAL	Information in the form of graphs and charts (eg pie chart, line graph, bar graph)	Good way to display information clearly, emphasise points and make comparisons (eg between monthly sales, company performance).
numeric@l	Information in the form of numbers (often as tables and spreadsheets)	Allows an organisation to make financial predictions, perform calculations and analyse its financial performance, especially if using a spreadsheet.
Quantitative MEASURED *i* NUMBERS	Information that can be measured and which is normally expressed in numerical form	Helps an organisation to analyse information and make accurate forecasts.
Qualitative JUDGEMENT *i* WORDS	Information that is expressed in words and is descriptive, and involves judgements or opinions	Allows an organisation to find out people's opinions about, for example, its products, advertising and new initiatives. However, this information can be biased and may be difficult to analyse.

(Higher)

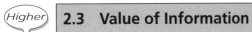

2.3 Value of Information

(Higher)

To be effective, decision-making must make use of high quality information. High quality information, with value to the user, has the following characteristics:

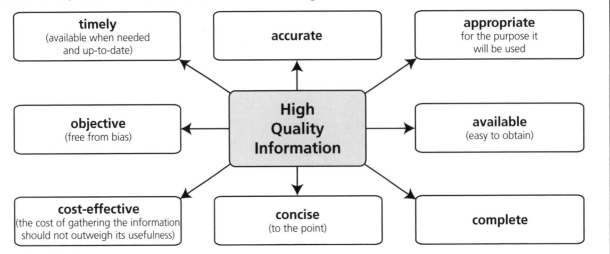

- **timely** (available when needed and up-to-date)
- **accurate**
- **appropriate** for the purpose it will be used
- **objective** (free from bias)
- **High Quality Information**
- **available** (easy to obtain)
- **cost-effective** (the cost of gathering the information should not outweigh its usefulness)
- **concise** (to the point)
- **complete**

2.4 Uses of Information in Business

Information is useful in business because it

helps monitor and control the business
Information helps to ensure that the business is running smoothly and helps to check progress so that action can be taken if problems are highlighted. Internal information such as budgets and production/sales records is especially useful.

assists in decision-making
Owners and managers of a business have to make many decisions (including wage rates, product prices, suppliers and the number of people to hire) and they need quality information to do this.

measures performance
Owners and managers must evaluate how the business is performing financially (eg in meeting sales and production targets). Information must therefore be gathered to assist with this evaluation.

identifies new business opportunities
Owners and managers must be aware of and collect information to identify any new or changing opportunities to be involved in. They may want to collect written and oral information from primary and secondary sources to assist with this.

2.5 Types of IT

Type of IT	Strengths and Weaknesses
Mainframe Computers	These are large, powerful computers that many users can access. They provide database access and file storage. Call centres use mainframe computers with users gaining access to customer files via computer terminals. These systems are very expensive to install and very powerful.
Personal Computers (PCs) and Laptops	A personal computer is the normal desktop computer used in homes and offices. Laptops are very easy to move about and provide flexibility for staff working away from the office. Laptops and PCs are still costly to purchase and can quickly become out-of-date and require upgrading.
Networks	Local Area Networks (LANs) link up terminals on the same site and allow information to be shared to each terminal. One of the computers in the network is the fileserver that controls the hard disk containing the data files. Information that may be of interest to many users is held centrally. Users access the fileserver as required, avoiding the need for duplicate files. A LAN can be linked via communication lines to become a WAN (Wide Area Network). Computers can be linked nationally and internationally.
Email	Each user has their own mailbox, similar to a postal address, on a computer. A user can check their box for mail and send messages to other computer mailboxes usually using the telephone line. Email has various advantages: • it provides instant communication • it is cost-effective as large numbers of mail items may be read, replied to, forwarded to other users, filed or deleted very quickly • the same message may be sent to many users at the press of a key. However, there has been an increase in the quantity of junk mail and staff may abuse the facility by sending personal mail which is costly in terms of staff time. Many computer viruses are spread via email.

Type of IT	Strengths and Weaknesses
Videoconferencing	This enables people in different locations to have meetings without the need to travel. A computer link is set up between people at two (or more) different locations, who can then meet via computer to speak to and see each other. Videoconferencing saves on travelling and accommodation costs. Less work time is lost through travelling. However, connections can be poor or disrupted. If meetings are international then time differences can be a problem. There is a limit to the number of people who can effectively take part in a videoconference.
Internet	The internet allows firms to access vast quantities of information from their computers. They can advertise their products on websites, sell products to consumers, look up government statistics, use banking services and check information about competitors and new products on the market. However, it may be time-consuming to access suitable information due to the quantity available. Also, staff may use the internet unnecessarily so companies have to set up procedures to deal with staff who access inappropriate material.
E-commerce (part of internet)	Many businesses use their websites to sell their products and services to consumers. Their products and services are displayed on their websites and customers can order online. This allows companies to sell products and services worldwide and cut costs by having fewer retail premises and sales staff. However, personal contact with customers is lost and many consumers are still wary of purchasing over the internet.
Interactive CD or DVD	This is commonly used for staff training. It allows the user to control a video using a computer. The trainee watches the video and at certain points must decide what he/she would do next. The package responds in different ways according to how the trainee has answered.
Computer Aided Manufacture (CAM)	This is a technology used by manufacturers. It involves robots and computer-controlled machines in production. It saves on labour costs, produces consistent quality and does not stop for breaks or holidays! However, breakdowns can halt production and be very costly and time-consuming to fix.

2.6 Costs and Benefits of IT

Benefits of IT	Costs of IT
Increases productivity	Is costly due to cost of development, installation and maintenance, redundancy payments and retraining
Reduces waste	
Increases speed of work	Can create problems (eg between workers and management when introducing technology)
Improves accuracy as computers tend to make fewer errors	Requires new skills, often not manual, and staff retraining can often be difficult
Makes consistent production quality	Causes stoppages in production and inconvenience when IT breaks down
Saves labour	
Increases access to information	Can reduce level of staff motivation when workers are deskilled
Saves money as IT is often less expensive and more reliable than labour	
Saves floor space	
Improves communication and decision-making	
Improves working conditions as fewer accidents occur with new technology	

2.7 Business Software

Type of Software	Description
Databases	Used for keeping records of staff, customers and suppliers. Functions of a database:
	• Searches for specific information.
	• Sorts records into order (eg alphabetical or numerical).
	• Performs calculations within records (eg works out a supplier's balance).
	• Produces reports which summarise the information (eg a sales manager can search a stock file to print out a list of all stock items which are not selling well).
	The **Data Protection Act 1998 (formerly 1984)** covers information that is held on computers. Businesses that keep individuals', staff's, suppliers' or customers' data on their computers must register with the Data Protection Registrar. They must state the purpose of holding the information. Individuals have the right of access to any information stored about them, can challenge it and claim compensation if necessary.
	Companies which store information on individuals must:
	• process information fairly and lawfully
	• only hold information for a lawful purpose
	• hold accurate information and keep it up-to-date
	• not hold information for longer than necessary
	• install security measures (eg use passwords) to prevent unauthorised, inappropriate access.

Type of Software	Description
Spreadsheet	This is an electronic worksheet that is used to calculate amounts. Functions of a spreadsheet: • Performs calculations to provide, for example, totals, averages, and ratios. • Performs 'What if?' scenarios. By changing numbers in a spreadsheet the user can see the effect of this change on other figures. • Produces charts or graphs of its calculations.
Word Processing (WP)	This makes the creation and editing of text easy and efficient. Key features of a word processor include: • formatting commands (eg delete text, move and copy text, make bold, underline, use styles and sizes, spell-check, search and replace). • mail-merge – a facility that allows information from a database to be merged into a WP document. (Mass-produced mail which arrives through your door with personal details on it has been produced using mail-merge.) • importing and exporting text and graphics allows the user to incorporate into a document material produced on other software packages.
Desktop Publishing (DTP)	This is used to produce high quality, professional looking documents. DTP allows the user to import material produced on other packages and display text and graphics in a professional style.
Presentation Packages	A business can make professional, well-displayed presentations where text, graphs, tables, graphics or organisation charts can be shown by a click of a mouse button. The computer can be linked to an LCD projector to display a presentation directly onto a large screen.
Computer-aided Design (CAD)	This software is used by architects, designers and engineers to design products in 3-D on computer. Changes to designs can be made easily without expensive redrawing by hand.
Decision-Making Packages	These help managers reach decisions by analysing data held on internal company databases and records. It can also make use of external statistics and figures that are input into the computer system. The manager will query the software for certain information and the software then produces a variety of statistics and graphs to help the manager evaluate the information. A marketing manager could use this software to help him/her to price a new product, taking into account a variety of internal and external factors.
Project Management Packages	These assist managers in managing a project or team (eg a project to design and launch a new product). The software can be used to keep track of budgets, resources used, time deadlines and team members' tasks. The software can be used to print out progress reports.

2.7 Business Software (cont.)

Benefits of Software	Costs of Software
Information can be handled very quickly and efficiently. Speed and quality of decision-making is improved. Fewer errors are made when making calculations. Improved accuracy and quality of work. Flexibility of using integrated software. Savings can be made in staff costs.	Software can be costly to buy. Staff training can be costly – in terms of actual training and cost of work not completed whilst staff are being trained. Workers are less efficient/accurate until they become familiar with new software. Cost and time taken to sort glitches/errors with new software. Companies may have to buy new hardware to run new software.

2.8 Uses of IT

IT is useful in an organisation because it
- assists with effective decision-making
- assists with providing information for staff
- assists in maintaining accurate business records
- assists in effective communication within an organisation.

2.9 Effects of IT

Effects on Employees	Effects on the Organisation
IT results in greater productivity, therefore fewer staff will be required. Job losses result from resistance to change, tension or industrial action. Remaining staff may have to undertake retraining or updating of their skills to cope with the new technology – older staff may feel under pressure and may feel unable to cope with the changes. Relations with customers change with the introduction of IT. The growth of e-commerce results in dealings with customers becoming more impersonal, since contact is increasingly made through online websites and telephone calls. Staff do not have the same personal contact with each other. Contact through email is less personal than face-to-face meetings.	Introduction of IT and improved communication can lead to decentralisation in a larger company with more decisions being made away from its head office. Email and videoconferencing assists with this. Additional departments may be created in the structure (eg an e-commerce department). As IT results in fewer staff being required, redundancies and delayering may occur. As fewer staff are required, the span of control of managers may decrease.

3 DECISION-MAKING

Decision-Making

Making a decision means making a choice from different options.

3.1 Types of Decisions

Strategic Decisions
are long-term decisions made by senior managers. These decisions concern the organisation's strategic objectives (its overall purpose and direction). Strategic objectives often start with 'to improve . . .' (eg to improve profitability, to improve company image or to improve efficiency).

Tactical Decisions
are medium-term decisions. These decisions are about how to achieve the organisation's strategic objectives and are made by middle managers. For example, if an organisation's strategic objective is to improve profitability then a tactical decision may be to offer a redundancy package to staff to cut staffing costs.

Operational Decisions
are short-term (day-to-day) decisions made by departmental managers. These decisions are made when a change occurs (eg to call in a repair firm when equipment breaks down or to reorganise the shift rota when staff are ill).

3.2 Mission Statement

When senior management have decided on their strategic objectives they often let their staff, customers and suppliers know about these by producing a Mission Statement. This is a written summary of the objectives of the company, and is usually no more than one page long. It is often displayed in the organisation's reception area.

3.3 Decision-Making Process

Making a structured decision involves 10 steps that can be remembered using POCGADSCIE:

P	Identify the **P**roblem
O	Identify the **O**bjectives
C	Identify the **C**onstraints
G	**G**ather information
A	**A**nalyse the gathered information
D	**D**evise possible solutions
S	**S**elect the best solution
C	**C**ommunicate the decision
I	Plan and **I**mplement the decision
E	**E**valuate the effectiveness of the decision.

3.4 Influence of Managers on Decision-Making

One of the important skills a manager must possess is the ability to make good decisions. Most decisions in an organisation will be taken by managers at department, middle or senior management level. Senior and middle managers tend to make strategic and tactical decisions whilst department/section managers tend to make operational decisions. As managers make most decisions, organisational success depends very heavily on their ability to make the best decisions. Managers' decisions should be in line with the overall objectives of the organisation.

3.5 Influence of Stakeholders on Decision-Making

See Unit 1.8 (page 11).

3.6 SWOT Analysis

This is used in the first four steps of the decision-making process (ie in 'POCG'). It involves identifying internal strengths and weaknesses (ie strengths and weaknesses within an organisation) and external opportunities and threats (ie opportunities and threats outside the organisation). It can be used to analyse a specific person's, product's or department's performance or any other aspect of an organisation.

Strengths	Internal areas or activities in which the organisation performs well
Weaknesses	Internal areas or activities in which the organisation performs poorly
Opportunities	External areas or activities that the organisation could profitably be involved with in the future
Threats	External areas or activities of, for example, competitors; government policy; economic forces

Internal areas which may be analysed as strengths or weaknesses	External areas which may be analysed as opportunities or threats
Sales and Marketing	Political situation
Human Resources (Staffing)	Economic climate
Organisational Structure	Social or demographic changes
Operations and Production	Technological changes
Finance	Consumer tastes
Technology	Competitors
Management styles and structure	Suppliers
Products	Environmental changes

A SWOT analysis should be used to:
- identify and build on the business's strengths.
- assist with the decision-making process. The strengths and weaknesses sections help with identifying the problem; the strengths and opportunities and threats sections help with identifying objectives; all sections help with gathering and analysing information.
- correct any weaknesses identified.
- take advantage of opportunities available.
- provide measures to protect against threats or change threats into opportunities (eg people sharing MP3 files over the internet is viewed as a threat to music companies but these companies have now set up their own systems to provide a similar service, therefore turning a threat into a new opportunity to be exploited by them).
- make a firm proactive rather than reactive to changes in the business environment.

3.7 Costs and Benefits of Structured Decision-Making Models (POCGADSCIE and SWOT)

Benefits of using POCGADSCIE and SWOT analysis	Costs of using POCGADSCIE and SWOT analysis
No rash decisions are made as time is taken to gather information and analyse the situation carefully. Decisions are made using relevant knowledge of facts and information that have been gathered. Time has been taken to develop alternative solutions rather than jumping to the first possible solution. By following a logical process, ideas are enhanced because a range of alternative solutions will have been analysed.	Can be time-consuming to gather information and conduct analysis and could therefore slow down decision-making. Choosing from a range of possible solutions can often be very difficult to do in practice. A structured process can stifle creativity and gut reactions to problems.

3.8 Why is Effective Decision-Making Difficult?

Internal constraints	External constraints
Finance may restrict an organisation's ability to choose the best solution. Existing company policy may restrict an organisation's options. Staff may resist change. A company may lack appropriate technology. Decision-making staff may have tunnel vision, be unable to handle complex decisions, may fail to consult, or may be indecisive	Political factors (including government and EU laws) Economic changes Social factors Technological development Environmental changes Competitors' activities

3.9 What do Quality Decisions Depend On?

- Having managers capable of making good decisions
- Staff's ability to use decision-making techniques
- Quantity and quality of information decision-makers have access to
- Level of risk the decision-maker is willing to take
- Personal interests the decision-maker may have

3.10 Other Aids to Decision-Making

There are several other tools which can be used to help make an effective decision:

Brainstorming

This involves a group of people trying to solve a problem together by allowing all group members to state ideas that come into their heads. After all ideas are on paper they are discussed in turn. This can be an effective method of finding creative solutions to problems.

PEST Analysis

This involves looking at the external factors that influence an organisation:

Political factors
Economic factors
Social factors
Technological factors.

By identifying these, the business can develop strategies to take advantage of opportunities they throw up or develop strategies to combat something that threatens it.

Six Hats of Decision-Making

This is a theory that was developed by Edward de Bono in the early 1980s. When a decision has to be made, a person or group should look at the issue from all angles (represented by coloured hats) including their gut reaction, disadvantages and positive factors. If a group looks at an issue with a black hat on they should try to identify all the problems associated with the solution. The following hats should be adopted to look at an issue from all angles:

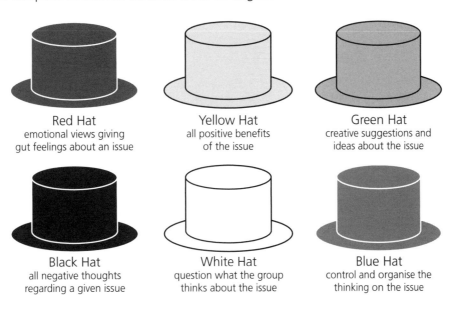

Red Hat
emotional views giving
gut feelings about an issue

Yellow Hat
all positive benefits
of the issue

Green Hat
creative suggestions and
ideas about the issue

Black Hat
all negative thoughts
regarding a given issue

White Hat
question what the group
thinks about the issue

Blue Hat
control and organise the
thinking on the issue

4 INTERNAL ORGANISATION

Internal Organisation

There is a variety of ways in which an organisation may group its staff and work.

4.1 Types of Organisational Groupings

Type of Grouping	Description
Functional Grouping	Functional groups are departments where staff have similar skills and expertise, and do similar jobs. An organisation which has functional grouping will typically have departments for marketing, finance, human resources and operations.

Advantages	Disadvantages
Staff with similar expertise are kept together allowing specialisation.	Organisation may become too large to be managed effectively.
Organisation has a clear structure.	It may be unresponsive to change.
Staff know who to turn to when they need a job done.	Individual departments may become more concerned about their own interests rather than the organisation's strategic objectives.

Type of Grouping	Description
Product/Service Grouping	Product/service groups are divisions/departments where each deals with a different product or product range. For example, a TV company could have a Sports Division, a Film Division and a Music Division. Each division has its own functional staff.

Advantages	Disadvantages
Each division can be more responsive to changes in its field.	There may be unnecessary duplication of resources/tasks/personnel across different products.
Expertise can develop within each division regarding its product/service.	Divisions may find themselves competing with one another.
Can give more incentive for staff to perform better.	
Management can more easily identify the parts of a business that are doing well and those that are not.	

Type of Grouping	Description
Customer Grouping	Customer groups are divisions dealing with different types of customer. There may be a different division for Retail, for Trade, for Overseas and for Mail Order Customers.
Place/Territory Grouping	Staff are divided into divisions, each dealing with a different geographical area. A Place/Territory organisation may have a Scottish Division, a North of England Division, a Midlands Division, a South-East Division and a South-West Division, for example.
Technology Grouping	This is a grouping in which a manufacturing company groups its business activities according to technological or production processes. This type of grouping is only suitable for large organisations which have different products and production processes.
Line/Staff Grouping	This is a grouping in which the organisation is divided up into line departments involved in generating revenue (ie sales), and staff departments providing specialist support for the whole organisation (eg finance and human resources).

Customer Grouping

Advantages	Disadvantages
Each division is able to give a service suited to its own type of customer.

Customer loyalty builds up because of personal service. | This method of grouping can be more expensive because of greater staff costs. Additional staff have to be employed to deal with a new customer grouping (eg if an e-commerce division was to be created).

Possible duplication of administration, finance and marketing procedures. |

Place/Territory Grouping

Advantages	Disadvantages
It allows an organisation to cater for the needs of customers in different geographical locations.	It can be expensive to staff, with administration, finance and marketing procedures duplicated in various divisions.

A business may use more than one type of grouping to organise its activities. A multinational company may use place/territory groupings by having a US Division, a European Division and a Far East Division. Each division may be split into functional groupings with each territory having its own Marketing Department, Finance Department, HR Department and Operations Department.

4.2   Organisation Charts

An organisation chart is a diagram that shows the formal structure of an organisation. An organisation chart shows:
- the relationships between staff
- who has authority over whom
- who is in charge of the organisation and each department
- the chain of command and lines of communication.

4.2   Organisation Charts (cont.)

Chain of Command
This shows the way authority and instructions are passed down vertically through an organisation. If the chain of command is long then decision-making and communication may be slow.

Unity of Command
If an organisation has unity of command, a subordinate is responsible to only one manager. This avoids conflicts which might arise when several managers have control over the same subordinate.

Span of Control
This means the number of subordinates working under a superior or manager. A reasonable span of control is from four to seven staff. The span of control depends on: the capability of the manager; the capability of the subordinates; the task being undertaken; and the procedures that operate in the organisation. A tall hierarchy gives a narrow span of control and a flat structure gives a wide span of control.

A Narrow Span

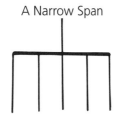

A Wide Span

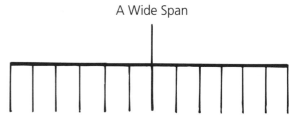

A narrow span means:
- the manager is able to supervise staff closely, which may put staff under greater pressure
- a manager may not have enough staff to share ideas with
- subordinates may barely have time to complete a task before the manager gives them the next
- there is a danger of interference by the manager.

A wide span means:
- a high degree of delegation is required which needs a high quality of staff
- there may be queues for the manager's time leading to delays in decision-making
- a manager will be under pressure to deal with everyone swiftly – snap judgements or poor quality decisions may be made
- subordinates may be forced to make decisions themselves when matters cannot wait for the manager and the manager may lose control
- the manager will have less time for planning.

4.3   Formal Organisational Structure

There are various factors which affect the formal structure of an organisation. These include:
- the size of the organisation
- the technology used within the organisation
- the market in which the organisation operates
- the staff skills within the organisation
- the products or services made or supplied by the organisation.

Organisations can be structured in the following ways:

Type of Structure	Description
Hierarchical	A traditional organisational structure with the organisation chart looking like a tall pyramid with many management levels. Decisions and instructions are passed down from senior staff with information passing back up. Employees tend to be specialised in departments and know their levels of responsibility and roles. Communication may be slow, resulting in resistance to change and inflexibility.
Flat	This is a low pyramid with few management levels. Information can be easily passed between levels. There are few levels of management and a short chain of command, giving more independence to each department. This structure suits small- and medium-sized organisations.
Entrepreneurial	Small businesses use this structure. Decisions are made by a few people at the core of the organisation. Decisions can be made quickly; staff know who they are accountable to and the decision-maker does not need to consult staff. This structure is difficult to use in a larger business and can create a heavy workload for the few decision-makers. It can also stifle initiative from other staff.
Matrix	A matrix structure can often be set up for part of an organisation when needed. A project team is created to carry out a specific task. Team members come from different functional areas. A project team might be set up to develop a new product, launch a new service or introduce a new IT system. Each team would have a specialist in marketing, finance, operations and R&D. Each specialist would report to the project manager as well as their normal functional manager. The benefits of this structure include increased experience, motivation and job satisfaction as staff can use their particular expertise in different situations. It is good for tackling complex problems. However, it can be costly to have a variety of different teams. It may be difficult to co-ordinate a team with staff from different functional areas. There can also be confusion as to who reports to whom as each specialist reports to two managers.
Decentralised	Control and decision-making is delegated to departments, which relieves senior management from routine day-to-day tasks. As subordinates are given responsibility, they are motivated and decision-making is quicker. This structure could be used, for example, by a retail chain with different stores. Each store manager would be responsible for the running and decision-making within her or his own store.
Centralised	Control and decision-making lies with top management in head office. This is often seen in a hierarchical structure. Procedures can be standardised for purchasing and hiring, for example. Decisions can be made for the whole organisation. It is also easier to promote a corporate image when procedures are standardised. However, staff who do not make the decisions have very little authority or room for initiative.

4.4 Organisational Relationships

Line Relationship
This exists between a manager and her/his subordinate(s). It is a vertical relationship in which work is allocated from the manager to her/his subordinate(s). The manager has authority over her/his subordinate(s).

Lateral Relationship
This exists between staff on the same horizontal level of the organisation.

Functional Relationship
This exists where a specialist function is given to a department (eg Personnel); that department is given responsibility for the function throughout the organisation. For example, a personnel department has a functional relationship with all the other departments in the organisation.

Staff Relationship
This is where someone (eg a Computer Consultant) has an advisory relationship with another member of staff. He/she has no authority over departments as he/she only advises.

Informal Relationship
These can develop between staff at breaks, during work and when socialising. This builds up a range of sources staff can seek advice from. Staff share information with each other and communicate regarding work-related (and non-work related!) matters. All organisations have informal relationships within them.

4.5 Changes in Organisational Structure

Type of Change	Description
Delayering FROM: TO: 	This involves reducing staff levels by cutting out levels of management to flatten the structure. This creates a smaller hierarchy where each manager has an increased span of control. Delayering helps to: • improve communication • make decision-making quicker and more effective • empower staff • cut costs as there are fewer management salaries to pay • allow an organisation to respond more quickly to market changes. Delayering leads to more responsibility and a wider span of control for the remaining managers. However, delayering also causes redundancies as well as giving fewer promotion opportunities for remaining staff.
Downsizing	This involves removing certain areas of the organisation's activities by closing factories or merging divisions together. Downsizing helps to: • cut costs and increase profits • empower remaining staff • become more competitive and efficient. However, downsizing may lead to a company losing valuable skills, experience and knowledge of many staff.

4.6 Empowerment

Empowerment means giving staff responsibility for their own work and decision-making by delegation, transfer of responsibility and greater access to information. This often occurs when a business delayers or downsizes.

Empowering staff may lead to:
- employees being more motivated and productive (as their work is not being checked)
- increased pay and training for staff
- enhanced promotion prospects
- decisions being made by the people who do the work, and so decision-making is quicker
- staff developing greater skills
- the organisation becoming more streamlined.

An organisation benefits from empowerment by having:
- good decisions taken quickly
- staff being more flexible and motivated
- improved productivity
- improved competitiveness
- more ideas on how to solve problems
- improved communication as fewer managers are required.

Empowerment may not be successful because:
- not all staff may want to be involved in decision-making
- managers may be unwilling to give up some responsibility for decision-making
- empowerment may come after delayering or downsizing. Therefore remaining staff may not trust the organisation.
- it can be costly to train staff to make appropriate decisions.

4.7 Corporate Culture

> *Corporate Culture is the values, beliefs and norms relating to the company or organisation that are shared by all its staff.*

Corporate culture is developed through:
- the ideals and principles of the founder, owners or senior management
- the use of symbols, logos, mottoes, uniforms, shop layouts and examples of outstanding employees.

Communication of Corporate Culture
Staff have to be made aware of the corporate culture. This can, for example, be done through: honouring employees for excellent work, training courses, company magazines/newsletters, company events, social events, staff uniforms and company videos.

Advantages of strong Corporate Culture
- Employees feel part of the organisation
- Increased staff motivation
- Improved employee relationships
- Increased employee loyalty.

5 MARKETING

Marketing

Marketing is the anticipation, identification and fulfilment of consumers' needs.

5.1 Role of Marketing

The marketing department of an organisation helps the organisation achieve its strategic objectives. These might include:
- to increase or maximise profits
- to increase market share (the market portion held by a business or by an individual brand)
- to extend the life of a current brand
- to become the market leader
- to increase the product portfolio.

Different types of organisations have different strategic objectives, which marketing helps to achieve. For example:
- a local authority may want to increase public use of certain facilities
- a charity may want to increase donations or raise awareness of the plight of others
- the police may want to raise awareness of certain campaigns and reduce crime figures
- a corporation may want to increase its profitability.

5.2 External Factors

Organisations (including their marketing departments) must take account of the environment in which they operate. This environment is made up of 'external factors', so called because they are outside the organisation's control. They include:

> **P**olitical factors
> **E**conomic factors
> **S**ocial factors
> **T**echnological factors
> **E**nvironmental factors
> **C**ompetitive factors.

See also Unit 1.14 (page 17).

5.3 Product Orientation v Marketing Orientation

Product Orientation
This is an approach to business where a company first manufactures a product and then tries to persuade customers to purchase it. The company does not conduct any market research before production commences.

Market Orientation
This is an approach to business which puts consumers' needs at the centre of the company's decision-making process.

The advantages for a company in adopting a market orientation approach include:
- it is more likely to produce products that consumers want
- it will be more able to anticipate and meet changes in consumer demands
- it will be able to make changes to its products or develop new products easily as it listens to consumers.

5.4 Consumer and Industrial Markets

Consumer markets are made up of individuals who purchase goods and/or services, usually from retailers, for their personal use.

Industrial markets are made up of organisations that purchase goods and/or services from other organisations to help them produce their own goods and/or services. These organisations are either manufacturers (eg soft drink makers) or service companies (eg banks and insurance companies).

5.5 Market Segmentation

This involves splitting consumers into different groups. Consumers can be grouped in many ways, including by:
- socio-economic group (eg A, B, C1, C2, D and E)
- family lifestyle
- age
- religion
- occupation
- income
- gender
- geographical location.

Market segmentation is useful to an organisation as it can assist with:
- developing **products** that are appropriate to consumers and highlighting gaps in the market
- setting appropriate **prices**
- ensuring that products are sold in the appropriate **places** for the target consumers
- ensuring that appropriate **promotions** are offered to the target consumers.

Niche Marketing
Companies sometimes identify a niche (gap) in a certain market. This involves aiming a product at a small market segment. The Whisky Shop, Starbucks and Tie Rack take advantage of niche marketing. Niche marketing is popular as it allows businesses to:
- build up expertise in one type of product and consumer
- avoid competition as niches are often not considered profitable by larger organisations.

However, companies which identify a niche and achieve significant market growth* often attract competition from larger organisations. They also have a high risk of failure as they rely on a small group of consumers.

* Market growth is the rate at which the whole market area increases. It is often expressed as a percentage. For example, if the tourist industry in the UK experiences a market growth of 10% per annum this year, 10% more sales revenue will be generated from tourists this year in the UK compared to last year.

5.6 Differentiated and Undifferentiated Marketing

Differentiated Marketing involves providing different products and services for particular market segments. For example, some car manufacturers produce different cars for different consumers – the Ford Ka is aimed at young, single, cost-conscious consumers, whereas the Ford Focus is aimed at consumers aged 25–35 who may have young children.

Undifferentiated Marketing involves aiming products and services at the population as a whole without producing different products for different market segments. For example, Heinz uses undifferentiated marketing as most of its products are targeted at the majority of the population. It does not produce one type of baked beans for AB consumers and another for CD consumers.

5.7   Market Research

> *In business, market research is the systematic gathering, recording and analysing of data about an organisation's products and/or services and its target market.*

Market Research can provide an organisation with information about:
- the size and nature of its target market
- the age, sex, income level and preferences of consumers
- the effectiveness of its selling methods
- what customers think of its products
- the effectiveness of its advertising and promotions.

The two Market Research Methods

Desk research is carried out by a researcher at her/his desk, using secondary information in the form of published sources (eg government reports, trade journals, financial papers, profit and loss accounts) originally produced by someone other than the researcher.

Field research is carried out by a researcher 'in the field' in order to obtain first-hand information for an organisation to use. The researcher goes out to the market and obtains the information her/himself.

Field Research Technique	Advantages	Disadvantages
Personal Interview involves a face-to-face interview. A personal interview can be held in the street or home (street responses are more brief, less friendly and less detailed than home interviews).	Allows two-way communication The researcher can encourage the respondent to answer. Mistakes and misunderstandings made during an interview can be dealt with immediately.	Personal interviews can be expensive as researchers have to be selected and trained. Home interviews tend to be unpopular with consumers.
Group discussion involves specially selected groups of people. It is usually led by an experienced chairperson who puts forward points to encourage open discussion.	Qualitative information in the form of opinions, feelings and attitudes are gained.	Can be difficult to analyse qualitative information
Telephone survey involves a market researcher telephoning people at home and asking them questions.	Relatively inexpensive The response is immediate. A large number of people can be surveyed quickly.	Many people do not like strangers asking questions over the phone, therefore hostility can be encountered.
Postal survey involves a market researcher sending a questionnaire out through the post.	Inexpensive as it does not require a trained interviewer	Questions must be simple and easy to answer. The response rate is very low. Consequently, incentives are often offered to fill in and return the questionnaire (eg free gifts or entry to a prize draw).

Field Research Technique	Advantages	Disadvantages
Hall Test involves inviting consumers to look at and/or try a product and then give their reactions to it. Often used by supermarkets when trialling new products.	Information gained is qualitative.	Can be difficult to analyse qualitative information. Results can be flawed because testers feel obliged to make complimentary comments about a product.
Consumer Audit is used by large market research organisations to carry out continuous research to monitor, for example, the buying habits of consumers, influence of advertising and effect of price changes. Certain consumers are issued with a diary and asked to record some or all of their purchases which are then monitored by the market research company.	Accurate information can be gained if the diaries are kept properly. Information can indicate consumer trends as they are completed over a period of time.	This is an expensive method to use as participants receive payment. There is a high turnover of respondents as filling the diaries in can be regarded as a nuisance. Diaries may be inaccurate or incomplete.
EPOS (Electronic Point of Sale) is used by retailers when Switch/loyalty cards are swiped through their electronic tills. Information about individual customers' shopping habits are recorded by the computerised tills.	Can give very accurate customer profiles. Allows retailers to offer promotions that are tailored to customers' needs. Assists with monitoring brand loyalty and the effect of price changes	Can be very expensive to set up the system to record consumer spending.
Observation involves a person being allocated the task of watching and recording particular occurrences or habits (eg recording the number of cars which pass a certain point on the road at a particular time to measure road usage and congestion).	Provides accurate quantitative information	Cannot ask questions that explain consumers' actions as there is no direct contact with consumers.
Test Marketing involves launching a new product in a regional area only. Reaction to the new product is monitored and if the product is successful in the test market, it may then be launched nationwide.	It may highlight particular aspects of the product that consumers dislike. These aspects can be amended before a national launch. Saves an expensive national launch if the product fails in the test area	Consumers in one area may have regional tastes that are not representative of the national population.

5.8 Sampling

When conducting market research it is often not feasible to question every potential respondent. A sample of respondents has to be selected. They can be selected by various means:

Random sampling – individuals are pre-selected from a list, perhaps the telephone directory or electoral register. The interviewer makes a number of calls to randomly chosen people from the list. It is expensive to operate as the people who have been selected must be interviewed – if they are not in, the interviewer must return at another time to obtain their responses.

Stratified random sampling – this makes a random group more representative of the population as a whole. The sample is divided up into segments based on how the population is divided up. For example, if the researcher knows that 10% of the population are in socio-economic group AB, 50% in C and 40% in DE, he/she will ensure that he/she selects 10% of his/her sample from the AB group, 50% from the C group and 40% of respondents from the DE group.

Quota sampling – the researcher is given instructions as to the number of people to interview and their characteristics (eg age, sex, marital status and income group). It is the job of the researcher to find and interview the people who fit the categories required. It is cheaper than random sampling.

5.9 Structure of a Questionnaire

Most market research methods use questionnaires. The aim of a questionnaire is to obtain meaningful answers from a large group of people. It should be short, simple and easy to understand. A good questionnaire must:
- have its purpose stated clearly
- have an easy-to-use layout
- have questions which are relevant to the purpose of the survey
- not rely too much on the respondent's memory
- be short, to the point and relevant to the subject
- start with a few easy questions to find out if the respondent is suitable
- avoid jargon, unfamiliar words and difficult concepts
- have questions in a logical order
- close with 'filter' questions (questions designed to place the respondent in a particular market segment, eg according to age, income or occupation).

5.10 Marketing Mix (The Four Ps)

Product	the goods/service that the consumer purchases. The product includes the packaging, image, guarantee and after-sales service (ie the total offer).
Price	the actual amount paid for the product/service by the consumer to the seller.
Place	where the consumer purchases the product/service.
Promotion	the way in which a consumer is made aware of a product/service and is persuaded to buy it. Promotion includes advertising, sales promotions, exhibitions and personal (face-to-face) selling.

5.11 Product

> *The product is the actual item that a consumer purchases,*
> *including the packaging, image, guarantee and after-sales service.*

5.12 Product Life-Cycle

The product life-cycle shows the different stages a new product passes through over time and the sales that can be expected at each stage. There are generally six stages in any product: development, introduction, growth, maturity, saturation and decline.

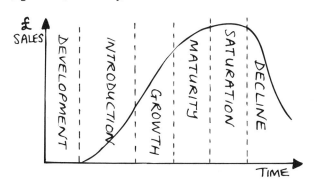

Stage	Description
Development	the product is designed and tested at this stage.
Introduction	the product is launched on the market. The costs of holding stock, advertising and promoting the product may be high at this stage. If the product is innovative, it will have few competitors and usually a high price.
Growth	sales increase significantly as consumer knowledge of the product increases. A few competitors launch their own versions of the product.
Maturity	the product becomes commonplace in the market. Growth begins to slow down. Competition increases and the price of the product falls.
Saturation	competition becomes fierce and prices tumble. Consumer tastes may begin to change. Not all competing products survive in this fiercely competitive environment.
Decline	consumer tastes change, technology changes and other new, more advanced products are launched. Sales fall, prices become very low and eventually the product is withdrawn from the market.

Some products, for example Mars, Persil, Heinz Baked Beans and Coca Cola, appear to never reach the decline stage. This is due to their having used successful extension strategies, having established strong brand loyalty over the years, having no close rivals and having established a high status in the market.

The length of the product life-cycle depends on the product. Car models have a life-cycle of approximately five to ten years; Furbies and cyber-pets had a life-cycle of a few months; and CD singles often have a life-cycle of a few weeks.

5.12 Product Life-Cycle (cont.)

Extension Strategies

To stop a product from entering the decline phase, companies often try some of the following extension strategies to prolong the life of the product:

- **Improve the product**. Washing powder manufacturers often produce new, improved versions of their products.
- **Change the packaging** to appeal to a different market segment. For example, Babycham was relaunched in the 1990s in blue bottles to give it a new, youthful appeal.
- **Alter the channel of distribution**. For example, the introduction of internet shopping.
- **Change product prices**.
- **Change the promotion and advertising**.
- **Change the use customers have for the product**. Lucozade used to be used as a drink for the elderly. It is now seen as a sports drink.
- **Change the name of the product**. A name change can generate considerable publicity and new appeal. For example, the chocolate bar Marathon was changed to Snickers, and Opal Fruits to Starburst.
- **Produce line extensions**. For example, Coca Cola also produces Diet Coke, Cherry Coke and Caffeine-Free Coca Cola, which are all variations of the original product.

5.13 Product Mix and Branding

Term	Description
Product Mix/ Product Portfolio 	A firm's Product Mix or Product Portfolio is the range of products that it produces. Baxters of Speyside have a product portfolio which includes jams, sauces, pickles and soups. By identifying the stage in the life-cycle of each of their products, a business can plan when to introduce new products as old products go into decline. Most firms have a range of products in order to spread risks. If a firm only produced one product and it failed, the firm itself would fail. A wide range of products can meet the needs of different market segments, increase profits, lower the risk and raise the profile of the firm. Some firms use the Boston Matrix to analyse their product mix. The Boston Matrix is used to place the products a firm produces into one of four categories:

		Market Share	
		High	Low
Market Growth	High	Star	Problem Child
	Low	Cash Cow	Dog

Companies should identify which of their products is in each category and then plan their marketing accordingly. For example, today's stars may end up being tomorrow's problem children or dogs, depending on the company's marketing activities.

Term	Description
Product Line	The product mix may contain product lines. These are groups of products that are similar. For example, Procter & Gamble manufacture a hair care product line that includes Pantene, Vidal Sassoon and Head & Shoulders. They also have product lines for washing powders, cosmetics and household cleaners, amongst others.
Branding	A brand is a name, symbol, design or combination of these given to a product or products by the producer which is intended to identify the goods produced. A brand may relate to an individual product (eg Persil), or a whole company (eg Heinz). Some brands are so powerful that they are in everyday use to describe a product, such as Hoover, Tippex and Sellotape.
	A manufacturer of a successful brand can save money on marketing, higher prices can be charged and consumers may become brand loyal. It also becomes easier to launch new products with the same brand name.
	Brands often require a high level of advertising and research and development costs to maintain a high public profile. A poor brand may affect the whole range of products produced by the one manufacturer.
	A consumer may see a brand as a guarantee of quality. A brand is easily recognisable. There may be 'snob value' in a consumer using certain brands. However, some brands cost more as consumers are paying for the expensive packaging and advertising.
Own Labels	An own label refers to a retailer's own product which may be the retailer's own name such as Tesco Value or an exclusive brand to that retailer such as George at ASDA. The retailer does not normally produce the actual product.
	Own label products tend to need little advertising. Own label goods tend to be less expensive than other branded products but may be seen to be of inferior quality.

5.14 Price

The price is the actual amount paid for the product/service by the consumer to the seller.

Pricing decisions are especially important at certain times, for example when introducing new products, when the product life-cycle is to be extended, when placing existing products into a new market and during periods of rising costs. Pricing decisions are also made when competitors change their prices, when competitors alter other aspects of their marketing mix and when balancing prices between individual products in a product line.

5.14 Price (cont.)

Overall, the price a company charges for a product should be based on what the customer is prepared to pay for it. This is dependent on:

- the company's objectives
- competitors' prices
- the position of the product in its life-cycle
- the cost of manufacturing the product
- the time of year – if the company offers summer/Christmas sales or if the product is seasonal
- the level of advertising and promotion
- the profit level expected
- suppliers' prices
- the market segment the product is aimed at
- the place where the product is sold
- the state of the economy (eg in a recession prices may fall)
- government pressure (eg car manufacturers reduced some prices following government pressure).

5.15 Pricing Strategies

Type of Strategy	Description
Penetration Pricing	This strategy is used by a company that wants to enter a market in which competitors already sell similar products. The company will initially set a price for its product lower than its competitors' to tempt consumers to choose to buy its product rather than its competitors'. Once its product becomes popular with consumers, its price is raised to be in line with competitors' prices.
Destroyer Pricing	This is used by a company that wants to eliminate competition. Prices are lowered to force competitors' prices down. Weaker competition will be unable to survive and may be forced to leave the market. Prices then return to their original or higher level. This strategy can only be used by large companies who can afford to make losses until the competition has been eliminated.
Promotional Pricing	Prices are reduced for a short period of time. This strategy is used by a company that wants to inject new life into a product or reduce stock levels quickly.
Loss Leaders	Retailers often advertise a limited range of products at low, unprofitable prices in order to entice customers into their store. Once the customer is in the store, however, they will often buy other normally priced products and so the store will still make a profit from the customer's total purchases.

5.15 Pricing Strategies (cont.)

Type of Strategy	Description
Competitive Pricing	Some firms in the same market charge similar prices for products to avoid a price war. Some petrol companies, for example, do this.
Price Discrimination	Some companies charge different prices for the same product according to the time of day, year or amount of usage. For example, BT charges different prices for a telephone call at different times of the day. Holiday firms charge different prices for the same holiday according to the time of year.
Market Skimming	This happens when a company launches a new, technologically advanced product at a high price. The high initial price allows a company to make a large initial profit and recoup some of the research and design costs before competitors enter the market. As competition increases, the price will gradually fall.

5.16 Place

This is the route that products take to reach the consumer from the manufacturer.

How a product goes from manufacturer to consumer is called the Channel of Distribution. The following routes are possible:

The Channel of Distribution chosen depends on a variety of factors, including:
- **The product being sold**. If the product is highly technical and expert knowledge is required to sell it, then selling is often done directly from the manufacturer (eg mechanical equipment being sold to a hospital). In contrast, mass market foodstuffs are usually distributed through a wholesaler and retailer before reaching the consumer.
- **The finance available to the organisation**.
- **The reliability of companies in the chain**. If a wholesaler or retailer is unreliable in their part of the distribution process, a manufacturer may decide to supply directly to the consumer.
- **The desired image for the product**. When Häagen-Dazs was first launched, it was only available in exclusive outlets. When it had attained an upmarket image, it was made more widely available through supermarkets.
- **Government restrictions**. For example, certain medicines can only be sold via prescription in pharmacies.
- **The product's life-cycle**. If a product is in its introductory phase, it is perhaps sold only through more exclusive retail outlets where a premium price can be charged.
- **The manufacturer's distribution capability**. If the manufacturer does not possess a delivery fleet or a sales force then it may distribute through a wholesaler.

5.17 Direct Selling

Method of Selling	Description
Internet Selling	Many organisations now sell their products and services via the internet, taking payment by credit or debit card. It is attractive to consumers as they can order online from home, saving time and hassle in shopping. However, many consumers fear using the internet to purchase products as some sites are insecure regarding credit card details. Products are also often more expensive to purchase over the internet than in the high street due to the extra cost of postage and packaging.
Mail Order	These are goods sold to consumers through catalogues (eg Next and Kays). There is a large growth in mail order due to the convenience of shopping from home, often with credit facilities available. Companies save costs as few sales staff may be required and they tend not to require expensive high street locations. Some mail order products are exclusive (ie only available through mail order). Some companies who sell by mail order also sell from their own website. Some consumers dislike mail order shopping due to the lack of personal contact with the retailer and the high delivery charges. Companies may incur high advertising and administration costs. A high level of bad debt is possible.
Direct Mail	This involves a company posting promotional letters, brochures or leaflets about its products or services to homes and workplaces. These can be then ordered by post or over the telephone. Reader's Digest is an example of a company which uses direct mail. Consumers within certain market segments can be targeted. A company can also reach consumers in a wide geographical area. Personalised letters generated through mail merges can improve direct mail sales. However, some consumers do not like the vast amount of direct mail they receive – they call this 'junk' mail. Also, mailing lists of potential customers can very quickly become out of date so mail can go to the wrong people, costing the company extra money and possibly upsetting these people.
Newspaper/ Magazine Selling	Companies place adverts in newspapers/magazines describing and showing their product for sale. Consumers respond directly to adverts by filling in coupons to post, or by telephone.
Personal Selling	Some companies employ sales staff who sell products door-to-door or by telephone (called 'tele-sales'). For example, pharmaceutical companies employ sales representatives (reps) to visit doctors' surgeries to encourage doctors to prescribe certain medicines. Double-glazing and kitchens are also often sold by personal selling. Personal selling allows the product to be demonstrated, benefits and technical details to be explained and feedback to be received from potential customers.

5.18 Retailers

There are different types of retailer. Manufacturers decide which type of retailer to sell their products through.

Type of Retailer	Description
Independent Store	An independent retailer tends to be a small business, with one or only a few stores. It will often purchase its products through a wholesaler. The prices in an independent store will often be higher than in bigger chains as independents might not be able to buy directly from manufacturers and take advantage of bulk buying discounts. They tend to stock branded goods. Corner shops and the smaller clothes boutiques and gift shops tend to be independent stores.
Supermarket	A supermarket is a large self-service store selling food and household products. Supermarkets often purchase directly from manufacturers and can also receive bulk buying discounts. Supermarkets often stock thousands of different products at any one time, including food, clothing and music items. Supermarkets sell branded goods as well as their own label ranges. Safeway, Tesco and ASDA are all examples of supermarkets.
Chain Store	A chain store company has many stores with the same name in different geographical locations. They specialise in a particular type of product. HMV, Next, JJB Sports and WH Smith are all examples of chain stores. They are usually located in busy high streets or in shopping centres.
Department Store	Department stores tend to stock branded goods. They tend to have a variety of departments specialising in, for example, ladies' clothing, men's clothing and household products. They tend to be situated in prime city/town centre locations, and have an upmarket image. Debenhams, John Lewis and Frasers are all examples of department stores.
Discount Store	Matalan, What Everyone Wants and The More Store are all examples of discount stores. They tend to sell large quantities of a limited range of products at discount prices. Displays are kept to a minimum to minimise costs. Discount stores are usually not located in prime high street sites.

Retailing Trends

- Increase in out-of-town shopping centres. Most large towns now have retail parks or shopping centres on their outskirts. Many people prefer the convenience of having all shops under one roof. These centres usually also have food outlets, leisure facilities for children and easy parking.
- Extended opening hours to fit in with people's work and leisure times. For example, some supermarkets are now open 24 hours a day.
- Increased domination of the supermarkets. Large supermarkets now sell petrol, pharmacy products, clothing, music and electrical goods in addition to their traditional foodstuffs. With Wal-Mart having taken over ASDA, the trend of supermarkets selling a wider variety of products is set to continue.
- Increase in internet shopping.

Higher

5.19 Wholesalers

A wholesaler purchases goods in bulk, directly from a manufacturer and then sells in smaller quantities to retailers and other businesses. Examples of wholesalers include Booker, Makro and Costco.

Manufacturers sell products to a wholesaler because:
- it saves the manufacturer from making many small deliveries to individual retailers, therefore saving on transport, administration and sales rep costs
- it saves the manufacturer from high stockholding costs (as the wholesaler purchases in bulk)
- it saves the manufacturer from being left with stock if consumer tastes or fashions change
- it can save the manufacturer from labelling its product for retailers, as the wholesaler will sometimes do this for them.

However, not all manufacturers decide to use wholesalers. Some manufacturers decide to keep complete control over the way their product is presented to retailers and consumers.

5.20 Promotion

> *Promotion is the way in which a consumer is made aware of a product or service and is persuaded to purchase it.*

```
          ┌──────────────┐
          │   Aims of    │
          │  Promotion   │
          └──────────────┘
      ┌──────────┼──────────┐
      ▼          ▼          ▼
```

Persuading consumers to buy a product	Informing consumers about the product	Reminding consumers that the product still exists

Promotion includes:
- advertising (see pages 49 to 51)
- into and out of the pipeline sales promotions (see pages 51 and 52)
- public relations (see page 53).

5.21 Advertising

Informative adverts are used to increase awareness of a product or service and to inform the consumer about the product or service being offered. For example, adverts in the Yellow Pages tend to be informative by listing services offered; some Sunday newspapers contain whole-page informative written adverts for therapeutic remedies. Newly launched products tend to use informative advertising.

Persuasive adverts aim to persuade a consumer to buy a product by stressing that it is very desirable to have. Most adverts have a degree of persuasion.

Advertising Media	Advantages ✚	Disadvantages ➖
Television	Adverts can be targeted to a large national audience covering all market segments. The products can be made appealing by using colour, sound and movement in the ad. The product can be demonstrated. With regular adverts the product can maintain a high profile.	Television advertising is expensive. The product may not need to reach all market segments. The message can be short-lived. Many viewers channel surf when the adverts come on. New products, such as TiVo, allow programmes to be recorded without adverts.
National Daily Newspapers	National exposure can be gained. Technical information can be explained. Products can be aimed at certain market segments by careful choice of paper to advertise in. Readers can cut out and keep adverts for future reference.	People tend not to scrutinise daily newspapers. No sound or movement can be shown and adverts are often in black and white. Can be expensive to ensure a wide national coverage.
Sunday Newspapers	People tend to have the time to scrutinise their Sunday paper. Large national circulation. Sunday supplements are printed in colour, allowing adverts to have more impact.	Can be expensive to place an advert.
Local Newspapers	Good for targeting local audiences. Local readers tend to scrutinise the paper.	Often a poorer quality production than national newspapers.
Magazines	Colour adverts have a bigger impact. Can target a particular market segment by advertising in special interest magazines. Magazines are often kept for future reference.	Can be expensive to place an advert.

Advertising Media	Advantages	Disadvantages
Independent Radio	Cheaper to advertise than on television Can have a captive audience as listeners tend not to channel surf when adverts come on. Can target particular market segments by advertising on particular radio stations or during particular shows.	Listeners often do not pay attention to the adverts. Limited to sound only Reliant on the listeners' imagination for the advert to be successful.
Cinema	There is a captive audience. Adverts can be shown before particular films to appeal to particular market segments.	The message tends to be short-lived. Limited audience Some adverts for local businesses can be of poor quality.
Outdoor Media (eg billboards, sports hoardings and bus shelters)	Can attract a wide target audience. Often in busy locations – therefore can have a high visual impact. Passers-by will frequently see the advert.	Can suffer weather deterioration or be subject to vandalism. Passers-by may view it as part of the scenery and ignore it. Can be expensive to advertise (eg on football hoardings).
Internet	Can be relatively cheap. Adverts can target particular market segments if placed on the correct website. Adverts can be changed easily.	Limited audience. Web surfers may ignore adverts.
Direct Mail	Can target particular market segments.	Consumers tend to dislike junk mail. Need to target mail accurately to intended consumers otherwise little interest will be generated in the product.

Product endorsement occurs when famous sports or showbiz personalities are paid to wear and use a particular product. For example, Adidas pay David Beckham and Nike pay Tiger Woods to wear their products.

Product placement involves a firm paying for its products to be used in films or TV programmes. For example, BMW paid for James Bond to be seen driving its cars in *Goldeneye*, *Tomorrow Never Dies* and *The World is Not Enough*.

5.21 Advertising (cont.)

The choice of advertising media depends on:
- the product to be advertised
- the market segment to be targeted
- the type of coverage required (national or local)
- the advertising budget available
- how competitors advertise their products
- how technical the product is
- the size of the organisation
- legal restrictions (eg tobacco products cannot be advertised on TV).

Controls on Advertising
The *Advertising Standards Authority (ASA)* is an organisation that monitors non-broadcast advertising, sales, promotions and direct marketing. It covers newspapers, magazines, billboards, text messages and internet banner adverts. If an advert is found to be offensive or untruthful, the ASA can ask the advertiser to withdraw or amend the advert.

Ofcom monitors TV and radio advertising.

The *Trades Description Act 1968* states that a product must be advertised in an honest way which is not misleading to consumers.

5.22 Sales Promotions

> *Sales promotions are short-term inducements used to encourage sales.*

There are two groups of sales promotion:

Into the Pipeline Promotions
These are offered by manufacturers to retailers (dealers) to encourage them to stock their products:

- point of sale displays
- dealer loaders
- sale or return
- dealer competitions/bonuses
- staff training
- credit facilities.

Out of the Pipeline Promotions
These are offered by the retailer to the consumer to encourage purchases to be made:

- free samples
- credit facilities
- demonstrations
- competitions
- BOGOFs
- bonus packs
- promotional prices
- free offers
- coupons/vouchers
- premium offers.

Into the Pipeline Promotions	Out of the Pipeline Promotions
Point of sale materials such as posters, racks to hold videos or leaflets, window display materials or in-store displays are often provided free of charge. For example, Disneyland Paris provides UK travel agents with boards and posters to use as window displays advertising Disneyland Paris.	**Free samples** are often used to encourage purchase. For example, hair care companies frequently attach a free sample of a conditioner to their shampoos.
Dealer loaders are used as inducements to attract orders (eg 'buy ten get one free').	**Credit facilities** are often given to consumers to allow them to obtain a product that they otherwise could not afford now, by paying for it at a later date.
Sale or return can be used to encourage a retailer to stock an untried product as it may remove the fear of being left with unsold stock.	**Demonstrations** at the point of sale involve giving samples to encourage a sale. For example, perfume counters sometimes issue samples of perfume, and car dealers offer test drives.
Dealer competitions can be linked to dealer sales with attractive prizes for the most successful dealer. Car manufacturers may offer holidays as prizes for dealers who meet sales targets.	**Competitions** in which consumers have to buy the product to allow them to enter are offered on the product's packaging, and in magazines and newspapers. Newspapers make great use of these to encourage purchasers to buy their paper by using, for example, 'Lucky Wallets', free holidays and scratchcards.
Staff training is often provided by the manufacturer if its product requires technical explanations or demonstrations. For example, car manufacturers offer dealers staff training which covers technical issues with new cars, how to promote the cars, and customer service.	**Buy One Get One Free (BOGOF)** is often used by supermarkets on selected products for a limited time.
Credit facilities often encourage retailers to stock a product. The retailer pays for the goods at a later date agreed with the manufacturer.	**Bonus packs** offer more of the product for the same price as the original (eg 15% extra free).
	Promotional prices are popular with consumers, but can be costly for retailers as many consumers would have purchased the product at its full retail price regardless of the discount. Supermarkets often discount certain products as 'Special Offers'.
	Free offers are often used by magazines where a free CD is given with the purchase of the magazine.
	Coupons and vouchers can be printed in newspapers, on the reverse of till receipts and in customer magazines. They allow consumers refunds or money off purchases.
	Premium offers offer with the product an extra product free of charge. For example, a free toy in a box of breakfast cereal.

5.23 Public Relations

Public Relations (PR) are the activities of an organisation which help it improve its image locally, nationally and internationally. PR includes giving donations to charities, event sponsorship, product endorsement, publicity literature, merchandising (eg providing corporate calendars and gifts), press conferences and press releases.

PR staff have the task of responding to bad publicity. To counteract bad publicity, a PR Manager often makes a press release to the media, either denying problems or accepting responsibility and so aims to create positive publicity to counteract the bad.

6 FINANCE

6.1 Role of Finance

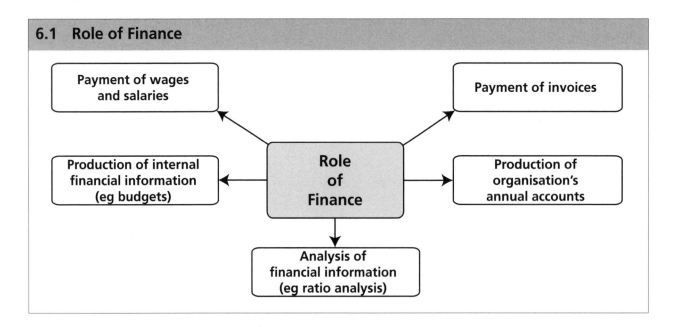

6.2 Annual Accounts

Financial records provide information on all transactions undertaken by an organisation. This information is gathered together and presented in annual financial statements, in the standard form of a Trading, Profit and Loss Account and a Balance Sheet. All public and private limited companies must provide annual accounts by law.

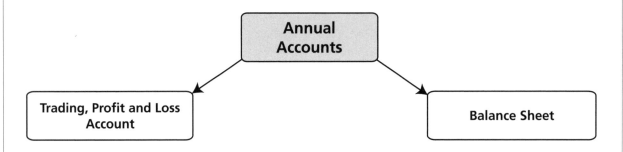

A firm's annual accounts provide a good guide to the profitability, liquidity and efficiency of the firm. A variety of groups and individuals use annual accounts (see Unit 6.6, page 59). Annual accounts assist with forecasting trends, monitoring performance and informing decision-making (see Unit 6.7, page 60).

However, its annual accounts may be difficult to compare accurately with another firm's accounts because each firm may use different methods to measure stock values and calculate the current value of fixed assets.

It is important to note that items which are not shown in the annual accounts have a major influence on the performance of the organisation. These include: the morale of the workforce; the technology used; the competition; the stage of each of the firm's products in their life-cycles.

| **Trading, Profit and Loss Account** | This shows the profit or loss over a period of time (normally one year). It identifies how much money has come in to the firm (income) and how much money has been spent and on what (expenditure). |

Trading Account
Calculates the gross profit or loss (ie the difference between the cost to the firm to buy the goods and the sales value of them). Excludes the firm's internal expenses.

Profit and Loss Account
Calculates the net profit or loss (the profit or loss made after all of the firm's expenses have been deducted from the gross profit).

Trading, Profit and Loss Account of Company X Year Ending Y	£000	£000	£000
Net Sales			100
Less Cost of Goods Sold			
Opening Stock		20	
Add Purchases		50	
		70	
Less Closing Stock		15	
Cost of Goods Sold			55
GROSS PROFIT			45
Less Expenses			
Rent		3	
Advertising		5	
Electricity		1	
Telephone		10	
Wages		3	22
NET PROFIT			23

A partnership and a company also have an Appropriation Account (given after the net profit) which shows how much of the net profit has been distributed among partners or shareholders.

| **Balance Sheet** | This shows the value of a business at a particular date. |

Items which the business owns and will keep for more than one year.

Items which the business owns and will keep for less than one year.

Items which the business owes and will pay for in the short term.

Shows how the business has been financed.

Balance Sheet of Company X as at Y	£000	£000	£000
FIXED ASSETS			
Equipment			40
Vehicles			30
Premises			100
			170
CURRENT ASSETS			
Stock at year end		15	
Debtors		30	
Bank/Cash		30	
		75	
Less Current Liabilities			
Creditors		15	
Net Current Assets			60
			230
Financed by			
Opening Capital			160
Add Net Profit			23
Less Drawings			−3
			180
Bank Loan			50
			230

Debtors are customers who have received goods from the firm but have not yet paid for them.
Creditors are suppliers who have sold goods to the firm on credit and to whom the firm owes money.
Capital is the investment that the owner has put into the firm.
Drawings are funds taken out by the owner from the firm for her/his own personal use.

6.3 Ratio Analysis

Annual Accounts can be analysed to highlight an organisation's **profitability**, **liquidity** and **efficiency**.

Ratio analysis is used to:
- compare current performance with that of previous years
- compare performance with that of similar organisations
- identify differences in performance to help decide on future action
- highlight trends over a period of time.

Limitations of ratio analysis:
- information contained in annual accounts is historical as it relates to last year's trading
- inter-firm comparisons must be made with firms of similar size and in the same type of industry
- findings may not take into account external PESTEC factors
- findings do not show the implications of product developments or declining products
- findings do not reveal elements such as staff morale or staff turnover.

Profitability Ratios

Ratio and Formula	Purpose
Gross Profit Percentage $\dfrac{\text{Gross Profit}}{\text{Net Sales}} \times 100$	measures the profit made from buying and selling stock. If the Gross Profit Percentage needs to be improved, a business may: • increase its selling price • find cheaper suppliers • try to negotiate discounts from exisiting suppliers • increase supervision to reduce theft or breakages of stock.
Mark-up Ratio $\dfrac{\text{Gross Profit}}{\text{Cost of Goods Sold}} \times 100$	measures how much has been added to the cost of the goods as profit. If the Mark-up Ratio needs to be improved, a business may: • try to negotiate discounts from existing suppliers • find cheaper suppliers • raise the selling price of their products.
Net Profit Percentage $\dfrac{\text{Net Profit}}{\text{Net Sales}} \times 100$	measures the profit made after the business has paid all business expenses. If the Net Profit Percentage needs to be improved, a business may: • try to improve their gross profit percentage • identify any expenses that can be reduced.
Return on Capital Employed $\dfrac{\text{Net Profit}}{\text{Opening Capital}} \times 100$	measures the return on the capital invested in the business by the owner or shareholder. The owner or shareholder (ie the investor) should compare the Return on Capital Employed with the return offered by other investment opportunities.

6.3 Ratio Analysis (cont.)

Liquidity Ratios

Ratio & Formula	Purpose
Current Ratio / Working Capital Ratio $$\frac{\text{Current Assets}}{\text{Current Liabilities}}$$ **Shown as: answer:1**	shows the ability of a business to pay its short-term debts. An answer of 2:1 is regarded as generally acceptable. If the Current Ratio needs to be improved, a business may try to increase its current assets or seek ways to decrease current liabilities. The Current Ratio can be too high. A high bank figure may mean that funds could be better employed in the business to generate income rather than sitting in the bank.
Acid Test Ratio $$\frac{\text{Current Assets} - \text{Stock}}{\text{Current Liabilities}}$$ **Shown as: answer:1**	shows the ability of a business to pay its short-term debts in a crisis situation. Stocks are removed from current assets as it cannot be guaranteed that they can be quickly sold to generate cash to pay off debts. An answer of 1:1 is regarded as generally acceptable.

Efficiency Ratios

Ratio & Formula	Purpose
Rate of Stock Turnover $$\frac{\text{Cost of Goods Sold}}{\text{Average Stock*}}$$ *** Average Stock = (Opening + Closing Stock) ÷ 2**	shows how many times the business is selling the stock it usually holds in the stockroom. The Rate of Stock Turnover may be too low due to slow-moving lines being held in stock or too much stock being held.

6.4 Cash Flow Statements

An organisation can show a healthy profit but have poor cash flow leading to problems paying debts on time and paying dividends. A cash flow statement is produced by a company in addition to the Trading, Profit and Loss Account and Balance Sheet to show the movements of cash into and out of an organisation **over the past year**. A company produces a Cash Flow Statement for inclusion in its published accounts that shareholders receive.

Financial Reporting Standards 1 (FRS 1) produced by the Accounting Standards Board provide a layout for producing a Cash Flow Statement. The headings used are:

- Net Cash Flow from Operating Activities
- Returns on Investment and Servicing of Finance
- Taxation
- Capital Expenditure and Financial Investment
- Equity Dividends Paid
- Financing.

6.5 Cash Budget/Cash Flow Forecast

A cash budget (also called a cash flow forecast) is produced for internal use within an organisation. It is a **forecast** of receipts and payments of cash. It can be produced for a few months or for a year. It should not be confused with a Cash Flow Statement (see Unit 6.4, page 57) which is produced for external use based on past events.

A Cash Budget can be used to:
- highlight periods when a negative bank/cash balance is expected. This allows appropriate finance to be arranged in advance.
- forecast surplus cash available as it may allow a firm to invest in assets for the future
- allow corrective action of anticipated overspending on certain payments
- make managers accountable for balancing budgets if each department operates a cash budget.

Cash Budget for June	
	£
Opening Bank/Cash Balance	1000
Receipts	
Cash and credit sales	5000
Commission received	500
Rent received	200
	5700
Payments	
Cash and credit purchases	3400
Wages	500
Advertising	1000
Rent	500
	5400
Closing Bank/Cash Balance	1300

Other Budgets
Companies can produce Production Budgets and Sales Budgets to plan production and sales. These may provide targets for departments to reach. They assist in co-ordinating production quantities that can be sold and allow sales managers to anticipate the quantity they require to sell. Managers should be involved with budget setting to improve motivation and make targets attainable.

Cash Flow Problems
Cash is vital to a firm. Without it the firm cannot exist. Firms can fail for a variety of reasons, one of which is poor cash flow. A firm can appear profitable but have no cash if too many customers purchase on credit and do not pay within the agreed credit terms. The business then has little cash to pay such expenses as wages, bills and insurance.

Sources of Cash Flow Problems	Resolving a Cash Flow Problem
• Tying up too much cash in stock. • Allowing customers too much credit. • Customers not paying within agreed credit terms. • Borrowing too much finance at high interest repayments. • Owners taking too many drawings.	• Offer discounts and promotions to encourage cash sales and reduce stock levels. • Sell any unnecessary fixed assets. • Encourage overdue customers to pay their bills. • Arrange credit with suppliers. • Seek another source of finance (eg find a partner). • Owners draw less.

6.6 Users of Financial Information

There is a variety of individuals, groups and organisations that use an organisation's financial information. These include:

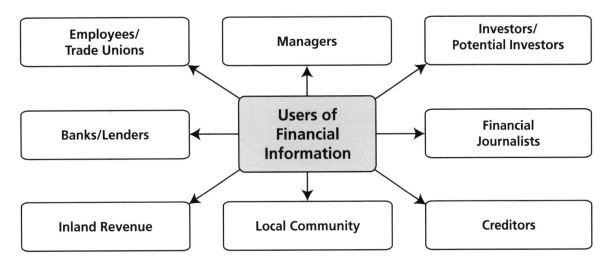

User	Interest in an Organisation's Financial Information
Managers	Managers use profitability ratios to check on the organisation's performance in comparison to previous years and competitors. They seek ways to improve the profitability of their organisation for the future. They attempt to identify areas where savings could be made and costs reduced.
Investors/ Potential Investors	Investors are interested in the profitability ratios, especially the Return on Capital Employed. They compare the return from their investment with other investment opportunities.
Financial Journalists	These journalists use the annual accounts and any other information about an organisation to assess its performance, for inclusion in the financial pages of the national newspapers.
Creditors	Creditors are interested in the overall profitability of an organisation. They are especially interested in the liquidity ratios to assess the likelihood of receiving payment for goods they have supplied or intend to supply to an organisation.
Inland Revenue	This government department is especially interested in the profit made by an organisation. This allows the Inland Revenue to calculate tax due from the organisation.
Banks/ Lenders	Banks and other lenders assess the overall profitability of an organisation. They are also interested in the liquidity of an organisation to decide whether to supply finance or demand repayment of amounts already loaned. They will also analyse the existing level of debt the organisation has.
Employees/ Trade Unions	Employees and trade unions assess the profitability of an organisation in order to determine suitable wage/salary increases that they may be entitled to. They may also be interested in the liquidity and sales revenue of the organisation to assess their own and their members' job security.
Local Community	If an organisation is in trouble financially and closes down, the economy of the local community (especially employment) will be severely affected. Local citizens will therefore be interested in an organisation's profitability to ensure continued employment and local economic growth.

6.7 Uses of Financial Information

Use of Information	Benefit
To control costs and expenditure	Financial information allows managers to identify where costs/expenses have increased in order to help them take corrective action.
To monitor cash flow	A business may be very profitable but have poor cash flow resulting in business failure. A business must pay close attention to cash flow to ensure that it has enough funds coming in to pay bills as they arise. Producing cash budgets assists with this.
To forecast trends	Managers analyse the firm's annual accounts over several years to help them plan likely future costs, revenue and profits.
To monitor performance	Managers use the firm's annual accounts to assess how the firm has performed compared to previous years and competitors. This allows corrective action to be taken if problems are spotted.
To inform decision-making	Financial information allows budgets to be prepared for internal uses. Budgets assist with decision-making and planning. Using ratio analysis allows an organisation to decide where improvements need to be made.

6.8 Sources of Finance

See Unit 1.12 (page 13).

7 HUMAN RESOURCES

7.1 Role of Human Resources

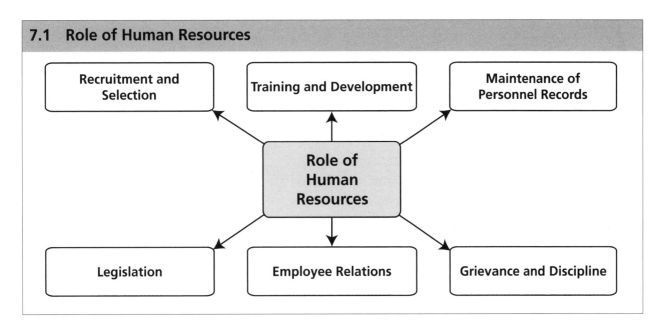

7.2 Changing Patterns of Employment

Decline in full-time, permanent work

Many organisations operate with a team of core workers who are permanently employed in either full- or part-time positions. When required, temporary, casual workers are recruited. Hotels, shops and offices often operate in this manner. The figures below show the number of workers in Scotland in full- and part-time employment over a period of six years. There was a general decline in full-time workers until 2001 when there was a large rise. There has been a significant rise in those working part-time.

	1995	1999	2001
Full-Time Workers	1,733,000	1,715,000	1,802,000
Part-Time Workers	556,000	570,000	576,000

Figures adapted from the Labour Force Survey 2001, Office for National Statistics

Increase in service sector employment

Traditional manufacturing industries have been in decline for a number of years, in contrast to a significant rise in the service sector (see Unit 1.3, page 5). For example, there has been a 29% increase in the number of staff employed in financial services from 1996 to 2002 in Scotland.

Increase in women working

There are now many more women in full-time employment than ever before. Many employers make special arrangements to make it easier for women to remain in employment by providing flexible hours, job sharing opportunities and child-care facilities.

7.3 Recruitment Process

> *A Recruitment Process is used by an organisation to find applicants for a job vacancy.*

Identify a **Job Vacancy**.

Conduct a **Job Analysis**.
Analyse the vacancy to be filled to identify the tasks, duties, skills and responsibilities of the position. This helps to identify the type of candidate that would be suitable for the vacancy.

Prepare a **Job Description**.
From the Job Analysis the organisation can draw up a description of the job vacancy. A Job Description states the job's title, location, tasks, duties and responsibilities. It can also state the conditions of the post including holiday entitlement, benefits and hours to be worked.

Prepare a **Person Specification**.
From the Job Analysis and Job Description a description of the type of person that would be suitable for the post can be drawn up. A Person Specification can describe the qualifications, experience, personal qualities and interests that an ideal candidate would possess.

Advertise the job vacancy.
A job advert can be drawn up using the Job Description and Person Specification.

Internal Sources   **External Sources**

Internal Sources	Jobs can be advertised internally within an organisation through a staff newsletter, notice or bulletin board. This method of recruitment is often used when internal restructuring is taking place.
	This can be an efficient method of recruitment: the vacancy can be filled quickly; it can enhance company morale if a company is known to promote from within; the employer will know the past record of applicants; and the company can save on induction and training costs.
	However, applicants are drawn from a limited pool of potential candidates. Also, as one vacancy is filled, another will require filling.

7.3 Recruitment Process (cont.)

External Sources	External recruitment allows an organisation to appoint someone from outside the organisation who can bring new ideas and experience to a job. It may avoid jealousy that might exist between rival internal candidates.
	Newspaper Adverts National or local papers can be used depending on the vacancy. National adverts can be expensive to place but they do reach a wide target audience.
	Specialist Magazines/Journals For example, teaching posts are advertised in TES (the *Times Educational Supplement*); agriculture-related jobs are advertised in *The Scottish Farmer*. By advertising in such magazines and journals employers can easily target potential candidates with the correct qualifications.
	Internet Adverts Vacancies can be advertised over the internet on particular company websites or on specialist recruitment websites. However, the advert may only reach a limited number of potential candidates.
	Job Centre Local vacancies (eg for office, hotel and manual workers) are often advertised in job centres.
	Recruitment Agency Potential candidates can register with a private recruitment agency. When an employer contacts the agency with a vacancy to be filled, the agency selects candidates from those registered with it for the employer to interview. The agency will receive payment from the employer when it supplies a successful applicant for the vacancy. This process can save an employer advertising costs and can allow staff to be recruited quickly, especially for temporary posts.
	Schools/Colleges/Universities Employers may contact educational institutions directly to seek young applicants who have the potential to become assets to the company.

7.4 Selection Process

A Selection Process is used by an organisation to select the best candidate for the vacancy.

Application Forms/CVs and References

Application forms should be checked against the Person Specification to select suitable candidates for a vacancy. As it is normally impractical to interview all candidates, vetting application forms and references allows a short list of the most suitable candidates to be drawn up.

Testing

Tests can be used to provide additional information as to a candidate's suitability for a position. Attainment, aptitude, intelligence, psychometric and medical tests may be used.

Attainment tests often consist of demonstrating skills. For example, a recruitment agency for temporary office staff may give applicants a word-processing test to complete. The resulting words per minute counts will be used to assess their skills against a set standard.

Aptitude tests assess the natural abilities that candidates possess. For example, a candidate for computer chip production may be given an aptitude test that measures her or his nimbleness; a candidate for a financial job may be given a numerical aptitude test. The test often reflects the skills required for the particular vacancy.

Intelligence (IQ) tests measure a candidate's mental ability and may involve assessing a candidate's numeracy, literacy, thinking and problem-solving abilities.

Psychometric tests are personality tests where a candidate's responses to questions are analysed to reveal their personality and traits. There are often no right or wrong answers to questions.

Medical tests Certain employers require candidates to pass a medical before considering them for employment. For example, the army, police service and airlines require a medical to be passed.

Assessment Centres

Some large organisations have their own assessment centres where candidates are taken for several days. They may take tests including team building and role-play exercises and be interviewed. Candidates will be monitored to assess their social skills, leadership qualities and personality. Smaller organisations can still ask candidates to participate in similar activities either at their offices or at a hired venue.

Interviews

These are used to gather information from candidates by comparing their responses to criteria that successful candidates should have. It also gives an indication of the personality of the candidate. However, interviews can have limitations if a poor interviewer decides that a candidate is not suitable within the first few minutes and focuses on negative aspects of the candidate.

There are various types of interview:
One-to-one interview One interviewer conducts all the interviews and selects the best person.
Successive interviews Candidates have several interviews with different interviewers.
Panel interviews Several people will sit on a panel and the candidate has one interview conducted by the whole panel with each panel member asking questions about different aspects of the job.

The most suitable candidate is selected, offered the position in writing and given a start date. Unsuccessful applicants are informed.

7.5 Training and Staff Development

Most organisations now require staff to undertake training.

Benefits of Training Staff
- Staff become more competent at their jobs.
- Staff become more flexible.
- Staff motivation increases.
- Staff become more productive.
- Changes become easier to introduce.
- Organisation's image improves.

Costs of Training Staff
- Once fully trained, staff may leave for better-paid jobs.
- Financial cost of training can be high.
- Work time is lost when staff are being trained.
- Output is lost when staff are being trained.
- Quality of training must be high for it to have a positive effect.

Induction Training	When a new member of staff is recruited, he/she usually undergoes induction training upon starting his/her position. This often covers background information about the organisation, organisational/ departmental procedures, meeting colleagues, health and safety, and an introduction to the tasks of the job. Induction training is designed to make a new recruit feel comfortable in their job.
On-going Job Training	On-going job training can take place: • **on the job** – where training is conducted at the employee's normal place of work. • **off the job** – where training is conducted at a different location from the normal place of work such as at the company's training centre, college/university or training provider's centre. **Training Methods**

Demonstration	The trainee watches a task being demonstrated, then completes it themselves.
Coaching	The trainee is taken through a task step by step and helped to improve by a trainer or coach.
Job Rotation	The trainee moves around different jobs or departments learning different tasks in each. This is an internal method of training.
Distance Learning	The trainee receives a pack of materials to work through at their own pace. The trainee then sends completed work to an assessor to be marked or evaluated. This can be used by the trainee to gain an external qualification.

Staff Development	Staff often have an individualised plan of personal targets that they try to achieve over a period of time. The targets are often set as part of an appraisal system. Appraisal is the review of performance over a given time period. From the review, training needs may be identified. Employers also try to ensure they suitably motivate their staff. To do this they may: • issue bonuses and other financial incentives • involve staff in profit sharing or share ownership schemes • include staff in works councils and quality circles • have regular staff appraisals • organise team-building and social events • organise staff training.

7.6 Maintenance of Personnel Information and Records

The Human Resources Department keeps personnel files on each member of staff. It holds basic information such as name, address, designation and department. It also holds information regarding appraisals, training undertaken and promotion prospects.

Information may be held on the computer database. When staff details are kept on computer an organisation must ensure that it follows the Data Protection Act (see Unit 2.7, page 23).

7.7 Employee Relations

> *Employee relations are the formal relationships between employees and employers, which may involve each of their representatives.*

The main groups involved in employee relations are **Trade Unions**, **Employers**, **Employers' Associations** and **ACAS**.

Trade Unions	A trade union is an organisation that represents employees with regard to pay negotiations, conditions of service, dismissal, redundancy and other work-related matters. Different trade unions represent different types of workers. For example, the EIS (Educational Institute for Scotland) represents teachers, the NUJ (National Union of Journalists) represents journalists, the TGWU represents transport and general workers. The TUC (Trades Union Congress) is a body which is made up of representatives from most of the trade unions in the UK. Trade unions undertake **collective bargaining** on behalf of employees. If workers were to negotiate individually for pay rises and better conditions they would have little chance of success. Trade unions, therefore, negotiate on behalf of all their members. In representing a great number of employees they have a stronger negotiating position. Agreements between trade unions and employers can take place at a national level where an agreement reached affects all employees in the country, or at a local level where an agreement affects one particular factory or workplace.
Employers	Employers have a duty to undertake a process of negotiation and consultation with their employees and to keep them informed of changes.
Employers' Association	An employers' organisation which represents employers during negotiation. For example, local councils can be members of COSLA (the Convention of Scottish Local Authorities) which represents them or gives them advice during negotiations with trade unions.
ACAS (Advisory, Conciliation and Arbitration Service)	This is a service, funded by central government, that assists in disputes where agreement between employees and employers cannot be reached. It offers: **Advice** to employers, employees and trade unions on matters such as contracts of employment, personnel policies, legislation and any other work-related matters. **Conciliation** – at the request of management or unions it can intervene in a dispute and try to encourage a settlement that both parties will accept. **Arbitration** – disputing parties put forward their case and agree to ask ACAS to assess the problem and recommend a course of action to resolve the dispute which both parties agree to abide by. ACAS is often involved in disputes that are heading towards an industrial tribunal. An industrial tribunal is a legal court that deals with all work-related disputes including unfair dismissal, discrimination and equal pay cases.

> *To promote positive employee relations, an organisation should involve itself in negotiation, consultation and arbitration.*

Negotiation
This occurs when employees and employers jointly discuss matters that are of concern to them in an attempt to reach an amicable agreement. Negotiation often takes place using collective bargaining and usually involves compromise by both sides. Pay deals and working conditions are often agreed upon through a process of negotiation.

Consultation
When an employer wants to introduce change or new technology, they should consult their employees to ensure good relations continue. Consultation involves employers finding out the views of staff in relation to an issue. New procedures and definition of job descriptions are often agreed through consultation.

Arbitration
When a dispute cannot be amicably reached, an independent arbiter, such as ACAS, may be called in to give an impartial solution to the problem which both parties agree to abide by.

There are various ways to involve workers in decision-making and promote positive employee relations:

Worker Directors
Workers are elected by co-workers to sit on the Board of Directors to contribute to discussions. Worker directors have no voting powers or directors' privileges but express or communicate employee views directly to other Directors.

Works Councils
These groups are set up by an organisation and are made up of an equal number of employees and managers. A group meets to discuss any suggestions for change and any changes being introduced. Any major changes should be discussed at a works council before being implemented.

Single Union Deal
An employer may strike an agreement to deal with one union only, resulting in all employees who are union members being members of the same union. This makes reaching agreement easier. For example, at present there are several teaching unions that teachers in Scotland can join, including the EIS and SSTA (Scottish Secondary Teachers' Association). Any agreement on pay and conditions has to involve all unions. A single union agreement would simplify matters and make agreements easier to reach.

7.9 Industrial Action

When employees and employers cannot agree on certain issues, industrial action may be taken. Official industrial action has the backing of a trade union whereas unofficial industrial action does not.

Employees may undertake industrial action to force the employer to agree to a particular issue (eg a pay rise). Industrial action can result in lost production, losing customers and sales revenue as well as gaining a poor image and poor reputation. A company's share price may also be affected. Employers may undertake industrial action to make employees lose earnings and weaken their resolve. Employers may also threaten employees with redundancy if they do not agree to their terms.

Employee Action	Employer Action
• **Sit in** Employees remain at the workplace but do no work. • **Overtime ban** Employees refuse to work overtime requested by employer. • **Work to rule** Employees only undertake tasks stated in their job descriptions. • **Go slow** Employees produce work at a slower rate. • **Strike** Last resort action where workers refuse to enter work. This is often accompanied by demonstrations, marches and a picket line.	• **Withdrawal of overtime** Employer removes the opportunity for employees to work overtime. • **Lock out** Employees are locked out of the business premises. • **Close** Last resort action where a factory or workplace is closed and relocated. This results in redundancy for the existing workforce.

7.10 Legislation

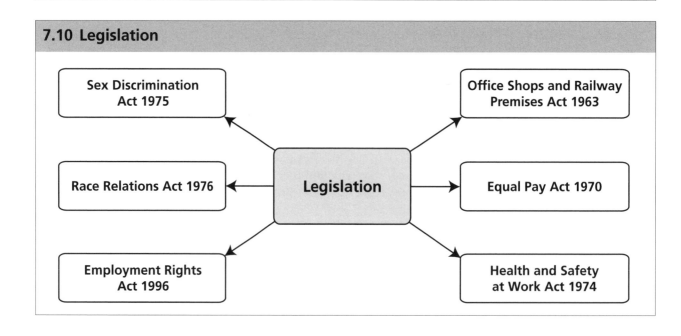

7.10 Legislation (cont.)

Equality Legislation	**Equal Pay Act 1970** This states that all employees should receive the same rate of pay where work of 'equal value' is undertaken. Jobs do not need to be identical but require the same skills, expertise and qualifications to be regarded as of 'equal value'. Equality in bonuses, holidays, sick leave and other benefits must also be maintained. Each of the following pieces of legislation makes it unlawful to discriminate regarding recruitment, promotions, terms of conditions of employment and dismissal. **Sex Discrimination Act 1975** This prohibits discrimination on the grounds of sex or marital status. **Race Relations Act 1976** This prohibits discrimination on the grounds of race, colour, nationality or ethnic origin. **Disability Discrimination Act 1995** This prohibits discrimination against disabled pesons. Employers have a duty to make reasonable adjustments to the workplace to accomodate staff with disabilities. **Employment Equality (Religion or belief) Regulations 2003** This prohibits discrimination on the grounds of religion or belief.
Employment Rights Act 1996	This states a wide range of duties and rights of an employer and employee. It includes the right of an employee to a written Contract of Employment within two months of starting work, the right to an itemised pay slip and rights of employees regarding Sunday working, maternity and termination of employment.
Office, Shops and Railway Premises Act 1963	This states some basic health and safety regulations that employers must meet regarding minimum: •working temperatures •toilet and washing facilities •first aid •space requirements for staff •outdoor clothes storage •cleanliness.
Health and Safety at Work Act 1974	This law added to the Office, Shops and Railway Premises Act 1963 by stating employees' duties with regard to health and safety as well as those of employers. Employees now have a duty to take reasonable care of their own health and safety as well as other employees'.
National Minimum Wage Regulations 1999	This states the minimum wage rates that can be paid to employees. There are two hourly rates, one for 18–21 year olds and another for workers aged 22 or over.

7.11 Grievance and Discipline

Any organisation should have a written grievance procedure. This should state the process that will be undertaken if an employee feels that he/she has suffered discrimination, harassment or victimisation.

An organisation should also have a written discipline procedure that should state the procedure to be followed when an employee has broken organisational rules such as inappropriate use of company email and internet facilities or theft. Procedures will often state the number of warnings that have to be given before fair dismissal can be considered.

8 OPERATIONS MANAGEMENT

Operations Management

This functional area is responsible for the design and implementation of systems which control the:
- **purchase** of raw materials
- **stock control** of raw materials
- **production methods** and **distribution**
- **automation** of the production process.

8.1 Purchase of Materials

Decisions have to be made as to how much raw material (the quantity) and from whom raw materials are to be purchased (the supplier).

The quantity of raw materials ordered depends on four main issues:
- stock of raw materials currently available
- duration of time which will elapse between this order and any future orders
- amount of raw materials likely to be required during this period
- storage space available and cost of storage.

Other factors to be considered include: normal spoilage during production; provision of some buffer stock; minimisation of stockholding whilst maintaining adequate supplies; the need for finance and purchasing to work together.

Once these issues have been considered, it has to be decided which supplier offers the best terms. The following factors should be taken into account:

- **Quality**
  Is the supplier's quality acceptable and consistent for the firm's needs?

- **Quantity**
  Can the supplier deliver the correct quantity?

- **Time**
  Can the supplier meet the firm's delivery date requirement?

- **Dependability**
  Is the source of supply dependable, is the supplier respectable and likely to stay in business, and is delivery reliable?

- **Price**
  Is it the lowest price; are discounts available for regular customers/bulk orders; are credit terms available; is it value for money?

- **Location** of supplier
  Are there additional charges for delivery or insurance?

Firms must use the correct mix of the above when deciding on a supplier and quantity. This is known as the **Purchasing Mix**.

> **Stocks include:**
> **Raw Materials, Work in Progress and Finished Goods.**

Having stocks enables goods to be available for immediate use in production or for delivery to customers; shows the range of goods available for production; enables customer demand to be met; allows bulk buying to take place to gain discounts.

Having too much stock can result in high storage costs; high maintenance costs; high security costs; high insurance costs; lighting and handling costs; a large amount of space being taken up; money tied up when it could be used elsewhere more profitably; stocks left unsold that may deteriorate or become spoiled; theft by employees.

Having too little stock can result in a business being unable to cope with unexpected changes in demand if its stocks are too low; if future deliveries are delayed the firm may run out of stock and therefore have to stop production; the firm is less able to cope with unexpected shortages of materials; firms holding low stocks may have to place more orders, therefore raising ordering/administration costs; out-of-stock costs (costs of lost revenue due to lost sales as customers cannot be supplied from stock).

Effective Stock Control involves the following:

Set a Maximum Stock Level (Economic Level)
This is the level of appropriate stock which should be held for the organisation to minimise costs.

Set a Minimum Stock Level
A minimum stock level is the level that stock must not fall below as shortages in raw materials may result in reduced output.

Set a Re-order Level
This is the point at which new stocks should be ordered. As items are taken from stock, the amount left for use reduces and at some point new stock has to be ordered. This is calculated by considering average daily usage and the time taken to receive new supplies (ie the **Lead Time**).

Set a Re-order Quantity
Once the re-order level is reached, a standard quantity is automatically requested. On receipt of the delivery, the maximum stock level should be achieved.

A pattern of effective stock control can be shown using the following diagram:

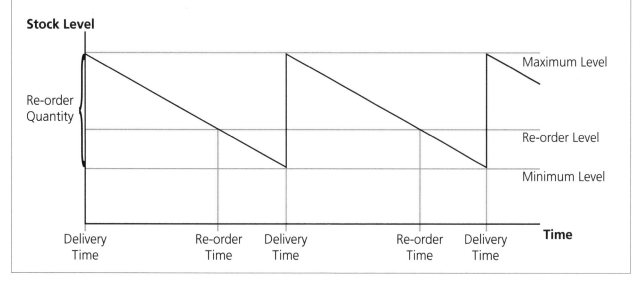

8.2 Stocks (cont.)

Control of Stock

It is often someone's responsibility to monitor, control and record stock to avoid theft, waste or shortage occurring. A general procedure which should be followed to allow stock to be monitored, controlled and recorded is:

- Materials should only be issued to departments after receiving a Stock Requisition from them (a form requesting materials which has an authorised signature).
- Stock levels should be recorded on Stock Record Cards or held on a computer database. These record stock used or issued to departments, and received from suppliers. Totals should match the actual levels on shelves.

Computerised Stock Control

Many organisations hold their stock details on a computer database. This helps to keep balances up-to-date after stock has been received and issued. Some are programmed to order more stock automatically as the re-order level is reached. Supermarkets use bar codes to help in stock control – as each item is scanned at the checkout one is taken from the recorded stock level. This allows the manager to check stock levels, total stock values and the store's sales easily at any time of the day.

Storage of Stock

Supplies of stocks can be held in one central storage area (centralised) or be located in the different areas in which they are used (decentralised).

Advantages of Centralised Stock Storage	Advantages of Decentralised Stock Storage
<ul><li>Improved security from loss or theft as it tends to be carefully controlled by specialist staff.</li><li>Specialist staff maintain stocks by following agreed procedures for its control – only issued when 'authorised'.</li><li>Central stock of components or materials may cost less to hold than many small 'on-site' supplies.</li><li>Improved efficiency in stock handling and management.</li></ul>	<ul><li>Stock is always 'at hand' when required.</li><li>Orders of new stock reflect actual production usage.</li><li>Speedier turnover of a small quantity of stock reduces the likelihood of its deterioration or decay.</li></ul>

8.3 Just in Time (JIT)

Just in Time (JIT) Production is a Japanese approach to production that involves keeping the stock levels (therefore costs) to a minimum. Stocks arrive just in time to be used in production. Goods are not produced unless the firm has an order from a customer.

Successful JIT depends on:

- reliable suppliers
- good quality control procedures
- access to a supply of skilled workers
- reliable workforce and methods of production.

8.3 Just in Time (JIT) (cont.)

Just in Time Production Advantages	Just in Time Production Disadvantages
Valuable capital is not tied up in stocks and can therefore be used elsewhere more profitably.	Danger of disrupted production due to non-arrival of supplies
Less space required for stock	Danger of lost sales
Closer relationships with suppliers	High dependence on suppliers
Reduced deterioration of stock or reduced stock obsolescence	No chance of quality control on arrival of materials
Less vulnerability to fashion changes	Increased ordering and admin costs
Reduction in stockholding costs	May lose bulk-buying discounts
	Increased volume of traffic on road (many small loads instead of fewer large loads)
	Increase in suppliers' transport costs
	Increased chance of transport failures

8.4 Kanban

This is another Japanese system. It uses markers, such as flags or lights, to order movement of stocks between different stages of production. If a flag is up on a stock item then it indicates that the item should be reordered. This is useful if JIT is to function properly to prevent a build up of stocks or parts in a factory.

Markers are used to tell the stockroom to take a part to a particular production line destination. If a production worker requires restocking of a part, he/she puts his/her flag up or light on. Markers can also be used to tell employees to begin production, to add their output to stock or to tell external suppliers to send stock to a particular factory destination.

8.5 Labour Payment Systems

A business can pay its employees by various methods.

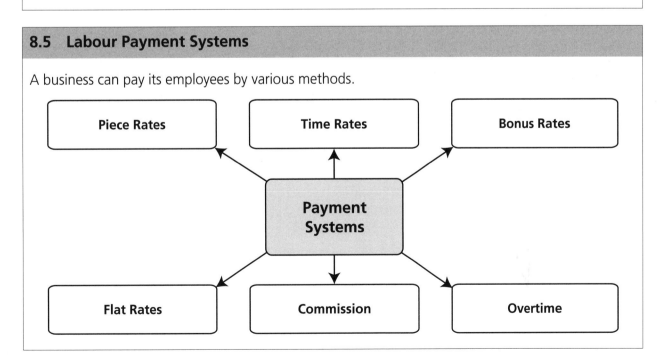

Payment System	Description
Flat Rate	Some employees are paid a set salary per annum. This salary is then divided into twelve equal monthly payments. Managers, supervisors and office staff tend to be paid by this method. It does not reward staff for a high level of effort but allows them a guaranteed monthly income.
Piece Rate	This involves workers being paid per item they produce. There is often a low basic flat rate with additional earnings made through piece rate. This method of payment tends to be used in factories. The more a worker produces, the higher her/his rate of pay. It can act as an incentive to employees to work hard. Close supervision of output is required to ensure that workers do not sacrifice quality for quantity. Employees may be penalised if quality is not maintained.
Time Rate	Many workers are paid per hour worked (eg £5·50 per hour). Staff in service sector organisations and manual workers are often paid at time rates. This method is simple to calculate for the employer and rewards the employee for the time spent at work. It does not provide any added incentive to produce quality work.
Overtime	When employees work a set number of hours, overtime may be offered for them to work extra hours. Their normal hourly time rate usually rises for any overtime worked (eg 'double-time').
Bonus Rate	Some workers are paid a basic wage with additional payments (bonuses) received when they meet agreed productivity, time-keeping and/or efficiency targets. The bonus is added onto their basic wage.
Commission	In many organisations (eg in some car showrooms and double-glazing companies) sales commission may be the sole method of paying employees or it might be added on to a basic wage/salary. Commission is usually calculated as a percentage of the products' sales value. It is used as an incentive by employers for employees to sell more. Supervisors, however, must check the sales techniques used by sales staff to ensure that they are not using rogue selling techniques.

8.6 Production

This is the process in which raw materials, components and finished goods are converted into new goods or services. A Production Plan is set which incorporates the objectives and functions of the whole business. Before production can begin, major decisions have to be taken regarding: plant layout; degree of automation; scale of production; method of production; and type of quality controls required.

8.7 Methods of Production

Methods of Production	Advantages	Disadvantages
Job Production is where a single product is custom-made to a customer's own specification. Bridges, wedding cakes and oil rig platforms are made using job production.	Firms can produce one-off orders exactly to meet customer demand. A high price may be charged. Specifications can be changed by customers, even if production has started. Workers are more likely to be motivated as there is a variety of work and skills required. Supervision can be easily carried out.	Expensive due to high skill of staff needed – therefore high wages. High research and development, administration and transport costs. A wide variety of equipment/tools is required. Lead times can be lengthy.
Batch Production is the production of batches (groups) of similar products. No item in a batch goes to the next stage until all are ready. For example, newspapers, bread and houses in a new estate are often produced in batches.	Batches can be changed to meet specific customer requirements. Reduced need for costly, highly skilled staff. Machinery can be relatively standardised, which reduces costs.	Machines/workers may sit idle between stages and between each batch unless there is careful planning. Expensive machinery may be required due to staff being less skilled. Stock levels may be high. Staff may be less motivated as they repeat the same tasks in batches. If batches are small, costs will still be high.
Flow Production is a process in which production items move continuously from one operation to the next. Each part of the process leads to the eventual production of the final product with the aid of machinery to save labour costs. Cars, bottled products and some electrical products (eg TVs) are examples of products which are often produced using flow production methods.	Costs are spread over a large number of goods. Therefore the cost per item is reduced (economies of scale are achieved). Bulk discounts are likely to be gained in purchasing raw materials. Huge quantities can be produced. The process is often automated, which lowers labour costs.	Huge investment to set up is needed. Individual customer requirements cannot be met. Equipment may be inflexible and may not be suitable for more than one purpose. Worker motivation can be low because of the repetitive nature of the job. Breakdowns can be very costly.

The choice of production method depends on:
- the product being produced
- the size of the market
- the size of the business
- the finance available
- the technology available.

8.8 Labour-Intensive v Capital-Intensive Production

Most manufacturing companies use a mix of labour-intensive and capital-intensive (machine-intensive) production. The actual mix used determines the degree of automation. The greater the reliance on machines, the greater the automation.

Labour-Intensive Production
Some manufacturers rely heavily on their workforce rather than machinery to manufacture their products. This occurs when:
- labour supply is cheap and readily available
- the product requires craftsmanship or special expertise to produce.

Capital-Intensive Production
Other manufacturers rely heavily on machinery and automation in their production process. This occurs when:
- a standard product is being produced with standard operations
- labour supply is scarce or expensive
- consistency is required
- continuous production is required.

8.9 Efficiency of Production

In order to monitor and control production, the efficiency of the production process and manufacturing workers' practices must be scrutinised.

To identify the most efficient use of production resources, a Work Study can be carried out. This is an analysis of the working methods, equipment and materials that are used in order to identify the most efficient way of doing a task or job. It is then possible to set standards of practice, to choose materials and to decide on machines and use of time. Work studies are carried out in two main ways:

Method Study
This provides information on how tasks are done at present with a view to improving practices for the future. The acronym SREDIM describes what a method study does:

Select the task to be analysed
Record how it is currently done
Examine the information collected
Develop a better method of doing the task
Install the new method
Maintain the new method.

For example, in a garage, a method study involves developing improved procedures for servicing cars.

Work Measurement
This establishes how long tasks should take so that standard times can be identified for each task. Actual employee performance can then be judged against the standard task times.

For example, in a garage, work measurement involves setting a standard time to be spent servicing each car.

8.10 Quality

Organisations in the UK use a variety of measures to ensure that their products/services meet a high level of quality. These include: **Benchmarking**, **Quality Control**, **Quality Circles**, **Total Quality Management** and **British Standards**.

A customer may view a quality product as one that uses a high quality of materials, has a high standard of workmanship, works perfectly, is reliable and is to the specification stated on the packaging or other product literature.

8.10 Quality (cont.)

If a business develops and manufactures a quality product, it may find it easier to satisfy customer demands, meet safety standards, and ensure the product works properly or can be repaired easily. The company may be able to charge a premium price and have a high status in the market.

Benchmarking	Identifying a benchmark is used as a method of improving quality of production or service by copying the best techniques used by another organisation regarded as the 'best'. A company which is the first to use benchmarking in its market will hope to be regarded as the benchmark standard in the future.
Quality Control	At certain points in the production process, products are checked to ensure that they meet agreed quality standards. A manufacturer passes a sample of their raw materials, work in progress and the final product through a quality control check. Any unacceptable products are then discarded as waste or sent back for reworking.
Quality Circles	These involve small groups of workers meeting at regular intervals to discuss where improvements can be made. Suggestions are then made to management for approval before being implemented. By including them in quality circles, workers should be more motivated, more productive and more willing to introduce new production methods.
Total Quality Management (TQM)	This is a system of doing things right the first time. No errors are tolerated. All staff, regardless of their position in the organisation, are involved in ensuring absolute quality of their work. Work processes are scrutinised. Teams/quality circles constantly strive to make processes more efficient and reduce waste. Commitment to TQM requires a clearly defined quality policy; focus on customer satisfaction; substantial staff training; constant auditing to ensure the process is working; teamwork at all levels; employee empowerment and a commitment from all staff regardless of their position in the organisation.
British Standards Institution	The British Standards Institution (BSI) is an organisation that produces national standards for certain products. When a business produces a product and proves it meets the agreed quality and safety standards specified by the BSI, the product will be marked with a BS 'Kitemark' symbol. This gives consumers confidence in the product because it has reached agreed BSI standards. For example, at petrol stations the BS standard BS EN 228 is displayed on pumps where unleaded fuel meets agreed quality standards.
Other Trade Organisations	Certain trade organisations introduce standards and logos that can be displayed on products that have met agreed quality standards that they have specified. There are Quality Assurance stickers that are displayed on meat products that have been produced to a certain industry standard. For example, eggs carry a red Lion Quality mark to identify that they have been produced to an agreed quality standard.

8.11 Storage and Distribution of Products

Storage

Most manufacturing or retailing organisations have to store stock. Finished goods are stored in a warehouse until they are dispatched to the customer. Some organisations have centralised warehouses in which all stock is held before being dispatched. Other organisations have decentralised warehouses where stock is held in smaller quantities at more locations, closer to the customer, before being dispatched. The type of storage used depends on the type of stock to be held, the finance available for storage, company policy, and the number, size and location of customers to be supplied.

Distribution

This aims to ensure that the right goods are in the right place in the right quantities at the right time to be sold. The correct Channel of Distribution must be chosen to ensure this occurs (see Units 5.16–5.19, pages 45–48).

The route through which a manufacturer distributes products is known as the **Distribution Mix**. This depends on:

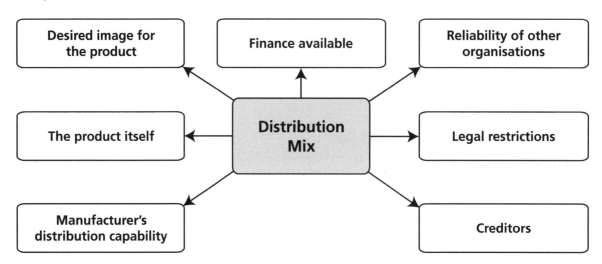

Products can be distributed via:

Road   Road freight (goods transported by road) accounts for approximately 80% of goods transported from one destination to another in the UK. The average freight journey is approximately 50 miles. Most foodstuffs and consumer goods are transported via road. Modern transport vehicles are often designed to transport particular goods (eg refrigerated vehicles transport perishable goods; car transporters are specially designed to transport cars). With an ever improving motorway network, road transport can be quick, efficient and cost-effective to use. It allows door-to-door delivery to and from any location, 24 hours a day.

Rail   The quantity of rail freight halved from the 1980s to the 1990s. It has since gradually increased due to increased transportation of coal and other fuel. BP, for example, are building a new rail terminal at Grangemouth to allow them to transport petroleum products via rail rather than road.

Air   Air freight accounts for a relatively low proportion of goods transported. Prestwick Airport has the largest quantity of freight traffic in Scotland. Transporting products by air is relatively expensive. Products arriving at an airport often also require road haulage to their final destination. Custom-made electronic products that require quick delivery outside Europe, are often transported by air.

Sea   Scotland's premier ports are located on the Forth Estuary. The main products transported via sea in Scotland are petrol products, minerals and coal. Sea transport is useful for importing or exporting bulky products but delivery times can be lengthy.

EXAM TECHNIQUE

The final Business Management exam has two sections:

	Section A	**Section B**
	Stimulus Material with questions	Extended Response Questions
Higher	50 marks	50 marks
Intermediate 2	25 marks	50 marks

General Tips

- Read all questions carefully.
- If you answer in bullet points be careful your answers are not too brief. Leave a couple of lines blank between each point to allow you to go back and explain your points.
- If possible, start each answer with a definition then answer the actual question.
- Check the marks allocated to each question. Include **at least** that number of points in your answer (ie if a question is worth 6 marks, write at least 6 points).
- Check the question several times whilst writing your answer to ensure you don't stray from the point.
- Allocate appropriate time to each section of the exam.

Tips for the Stimulus Material and questions	**Tips for the Extended Response Questions**
<ul><li>Read the questions first before reading the Stimulus Material.</li><li>Whilst reading the Stimulus Material highlight any relevant information (bearing in mind the questions).</li><li>Answer all questions.</li><li>Some questions may ask for solutions for the business in the Stimulus Material. Ensure your answers are relevant (eg if asked for a source of finance for a sole trader, debentures would be inappropriate to include in your answer).</li></ul>	<ul><li>Answer two questions only.</li><li>Ensure that you can answer all parts of the questions that you have chosen.</li><li>Include any relevant diagrams in stock, product life-cycle or product mix questions. Label the diagrams.</li><li>Give **explained** examples where possible.</li></ul>

WEBSITE ADDRESSES

There are many websites on the internet that can help you with Intermediate 2 or Higher Business Management. Below is a selection of web addresses you may find useful. We appreciate that addresses often change and therefore space has been left for you to include any additional websites you have accessed.

Unit	Information to be Found	Web Address
All Areas	Information and tasks	www.learn.co.uk www.s-cool.co.uk www.thetimes100.co.uk
Business in Contemporary Society	Information on franchises Links to all local and central government sites Entrepreneur Test Profiles of Scottish entrepreneurs Sources of assistance	www.british-franchise.org www.ukonline.gov.uk www.bizmove.com/other/quiz.htm www.localheroes.org www.dti.gov.uk/support
Business Information and IT	Hardware and software information Principles of the Data Protection Act	http://doit.ort.org www.dataprotection.gov.uk
Decision-Making	Example of a Mission Statement SWOT and PEST analysis information and tasks	www.benjerry.com/mission.html www.marketingteacher.com
Marketing	Marketing mix, Boston Matrix, marketing segmentation and market research – information and tasks Advertising Standards Authority – adjudications on reported adverts	www.marketingteacher.com www.asa.org.uk
Finance	Printable ratio analysis worksheets Links to UK company's annual accounts	www.bized.ac.uk (select Learning Materials, Business Studies, Packages of Resources) www.carol.co.uk
Human Resources	Selection: intelligence test attainment test Mock interview questions Printable pay, recruitment, industrial relations and trade union worksheet Information on TUC ACAS information and quiz Legislation	www.mensa.org/workout.html www.typingtest.com www.job-interview.net www.bized.ac.uk (select Learning Materials, Business Studies, Packages of Resources) www.bized.ac.uk (select Company Facts) www.acas.org.uk www.hmso.gov.uk
Operations	Printable stock control worksheet Virtual factory and production tasks British Standards information Best practice benchmarking case studies	www.bized.ac.uk (select Learning Materials, Business Studies, Extel Resources) www.bized.ac.uk (select Virtual Worlds, Virtual Factory) www.bsieducation.org www.dti.gov.uk (search for 'case studies benchmarking')
Your favourite Business Management sites		